A FAITH TO PROCLAIM

A FAITH
TO PROCLAIM

JAMES S. STEWART

*It is written, " I believed, and therefore have I
spoken "; we also believe, and therefore speak.
St. Paul to the Corinthians*

BAKER BOOK HOUSE
Grand Rapids, Michigan

Reprinted 1972 by
Baker Book House Company
from the original edition
copyrighted 1953 by
Hodder and Stoughton, Ltd.
London
Printed in the United States of America
ISBN: 0-8010-7977-2

Fourth printing, August 1978

TO

MY FRIENDS IN CONFERENCE

AT

YALE

PRINCETON

PITTSBURGH

AND

NEW YORK

PREFACE

THIS book represents the Lyman Beecher Lectures delivered in Yale University. It is my happy duty here to record my heartfelt gratitude to the Dean and Faculty of the Divinity School for their unbounded kindness and to the Members of the Convocation and all the students for the warmth and generosity of their welcome. To spend Easter week in such a fellowship was a memorable experience indeed.

A Lecturer on this Foundation is required to discourse on some aspect of the preacher's task; and I have chosen to focus attention on the essential message of our evangelism rather than on its manner or its method. Questions of sermon construction and delivery I have endeavoured to deal with in an earlier volume, *Heralds of God*, to which the present book may be regarded as a sequel. It remains to be added that, if the Christian message is to make a really decisive impact on the men and women of to-day, the Church must be prepared not only to preach it in word but to demonstrate it in life, not only to proclaim it from the housetops but to go down and incarnate it in social action and concern and in a compassion kindled at the flame of the charity of Christ. This is presupposed throughout what follows, and at one point and another I have sought to underline it. But it has not been possible, within the limits of five lectures, to develop this

7

aspect of the theme at any length. That would require another book.

To two friends my special thanks are due: to Mr. D. Craigie Pringle, who prepared the manuscript for the press, and to the Rev. Graham W. Hardy, B.D., S.T.M., who as on a former occasion undertook the revision of the proofs.

JAMES S. STEWART

EDINBURGH, *June* 1952

CONTENTS

CHAPTER ONE

PROCLAIMING THE INCARNATION

> To an open house in the evening
> Home shall men come,
> To an older place than Eden
> And a taller town than Rome ;
> To the end of the way of the wandering star,
> To the things that cannot be and that are,
> To the place where God was homeless
> And all men are at home.
> G. K. CHESTERTON, *The House of Christmas*.

TO-DAY as never before there is being laid upon the heart and conscience of the Church the burden of evangelism. Other generations have had their own specific tasks: confessional restatement, theological reorientation, ecclesiastical reconstruction. To-day the demand is more radical and basic. It is spiritual resurrection: it is—under God—the creating of life. To confront a bewildered and dishevelled age with the fact of Christ, to thrust upon its confusion the creative word of the Cross and smite its disenchantment with the glory of the Resurrection—this is the urgent, overruling task. "Son of man, can these bones live?"

There is, therefore, no place to-day for a Church that is not aflame with the Spirit who is the Lord and Giver of life, nor any value in a theology which is not passionately missionary. If there throbs through the Church the vitality of a living union with Christ—and apart from this the Church has no claim to exist, no right to preach, it is merely cumbering the ground—if the Church can indeed say "It is not I who live, it is Christ who lives in me," then the dark demonic forces of the age have met their match, and the thrust of life is stronger than the drift of death. A Church that knows its Lord and is possessed by its Gospel cannot but propagate creatively the life that it has found. A Christian who is taking his faith seriously cannot but evangelize.

I

The First Axiom of Evangelism

Now the first axiom of effective evangelism is that the evangelist must be sure of his message. Any haziness or hesitation there is fatal.

It is precisely at this point that the trend of recent New Testament study seems to me so significant. If I were asked what has been the most notable advance in New Testament studies within the past generation, I should reply—not the general solution now arrived at for the Synoptic Problem; not the exploration by Form Criticism of the tangled hinterland of oral tradition behind the documentary sources; not even the impressive and emphatic repudiation of the type of scholarship which, carried away by the influence of Comparative Religion, sought to interpret primitive Christianity in terms of Oriental dramas of redemption and to dissolve the faith in Hellenistic mysticism. Important as these developments are, there has been one still more significant. I refer to the fact that whereas formerly the focus of interest was the rich and wide diversity among the New Testament documents and the multiplicity of theological patterns they represent, to-day the emphasis is being laid on their deep essential unity.[1] And for a Church girding itself afresh for the work of evangelism, for a preacher seeking to "declare the whole counsel of God" to his people, indeed for every Christian who has a genuine concern for the coming of the Kingdom of God, it is immensely important to observe wherein this unity lies. It lies in what the New Testament itself calls the Proclamation, the message, the *kerygma*. For running right through the New Testament from start to finish, reappearing steadily through all the variations of Evangel and Epistle, Acts and Apocalypse, history and homily, pastoral and preaching, beating out like the deep recurring theme of a great symphony, there is the announcement—brief, trenchant and authoritative—of certain historic events of final and absolute significance, the mighty acts in which God had visited and redeemed His people.

Now it is not my purpose to traverse again the ground which many writers—notably Rudolf Otto, C. H. Dodd and Oscar Cullmann—have in recent years explored and made familiar. What I wish to do is to call attention to certain points at which this investigation of the apostolic *kerygma* has a bearing —a much more direct bearing than has yet been realized—on practical questions of present day

[1] This is well illustrated by A. M. Hunter, *The Unity of the New Testament*.

evangelism and on the ministry of the Word. It is beyond question that there is a real work waiting to be done in harnessing the results of recent New Testament scholarship to the Church's most urgent task. Here it must suffice to indicate certain lines along which that work should proceed.

The essential thing is that modern evangelism should be sure of its own foundations and remember the rock whence it is hewn.

What, then, was the nature of that message which, beginning at Jerusalem, awakened the world? Let me set forth its salient features; and thereafter add three notes on the content, the claim, and the communication of the message to-day.

Within the New Testament itself the framework of the apostolic preaching is clearly discernible. The general outlines of its structure stand out distinctly in the early discourses in Acts, in the Epistles (particularly in such passages as Rom. i. 2-4 and I. Cor. xv. 3 f. where St. Paul cites the primitive tradition), and in the evangelic records themselves, which (as the opening words of Mark expressly announce) are neither biographies nor memoirs, but representations of the redemptive activity of God, designed to win men for faith and salvation. It can, moreover, be shown that it was this same apostolic *kerygma* which at a later day determined the structure of the creeds and the liturgy of the Church.

What, then, was the essence of this proclamation by the original heralds of the faith? Quite briefly, it was this. They proclaimed that prophecy was fulfilled; that in Jesus of Nazareth, in His words

and deeds, His life and death and resurrection, the
new age had arrived; that God had exalted Him,
that He would come again as Judge, and that now
was the day of salvation.

This was the message. The main emphasis, it is
quite clear, fell on the death and resurrection. Here,
however, I would interpolate a *caveat*. There is a
fantastic idea which has gained currency in certain
quarters that the early Church was not interested in
the events of the earthly ministry of Jesus, and that
St. Paul probably knew less about that ministry than
we know to-day. This is absurd. The words and
deeds of the Master formed an integral and vital part
of the *kerygma* of apostolic Christianity, as they have
done on the mission field ever since. It is a quite
unwarranted assumption—based partly on a false
exegesis of II. Cor. v. 16, where Paul speaks about
"knowing Christ after the flesh no more"—that the
apostolic age was largely indifferent to everything
that preceded the Passion. There are theologies
which concentrate on the bare fact that God became
man, and profess to be quite uninterested in the
question—"What kind of man did He become?"
Such a document as the Epistle to the Hebrews, with
its vivid references to the human life of Jesus, would
be sufficient to refute this attitude; nor can it sur-
vive any but the most superficial examination of the
Pauline writings themselves. But there is other
evidence. One of the positive services of the school
of Form Criticism (and here I would suggest that
we shall be erring if we allow the extravagances and
critical eccentricities of certain representatives of

this school to blind us to its real contribution) has been to show how largely the selection of materials in the Gospel narratives was determined precisely by the usage of primitive Christian evangelism. It was not the written records that produced the *kerygma*: that was there before a word had been written. It was the *kerygma* that produced the records. Thus the general pattern of the apostolic preaching is clear. It told of the acts and sayings of Jesus; it told how in the purpose of God He had died for sin; above all, it witnessed to the resurrection.

The crucial point is that it was dealing with *events*, not abstractions or theories or pantheistic generalities, but concrete, actual events localized in time and space. Not "the idea of God" did the apostles preach, but God Himself in omnipotent action; not a "doctrine of salvation," but salvation, the living deed; not a *Weltanschauung*, but Christ. These men were not, like the Stoics, offering natural theology; nor ethical platitudes, as the Rabbis; nor mystical experience, as the priests of Isis; nor philosophical arguments, as the Alexandrians. They were not concerned to purvey moral homilies or religious uplift; they were certainly not advertising that familiar modern blend of legalism, humanitarian sentiment and cosmopolitan toleration which sometimes in this twentieth century passes muster for religion, but which in fact is less than useless in a day when resolute, fanatical forces of evil are out to envelop and enslave the human spirit in every land. I say *less* than useless advisedly, for an easy-going, theologically vague and harmlessly accommodating religiosity is playing into the hands of the destroyer of the freedom of men. No, the apostolic preachers spoke of facts, hard, concrete facts known beyond any peradventure. "That which was from the beginning, declare we unto you."[1] As Brunner has well expressed it, "Faith in Jesus Christ is not an interpretation of the world, but it is participation in an event: in something which has happened, which is happening, and which is going to happen."[2]

II

FACTS OF HISTORY

Now the particular facts enshrined in the early preaching can be characterized in three ways.

They were, first, *historic* facts—as distinct from facts of nature, or facts of intuition or rational deduction or mystical experience. It was indeed pre-eminently the "age of the Spirit": but it had simply nothing in common with the idealism which, regarding involvement in history as indicating a stage of rudimentary religious development and intellectual triviality, of anthropomorphism and mythology and defective spirituality, seeks to escape beyond history into the freedom of timeless, transcendent, disincarnate truth—thus making itself more spiritual than God. For the Spirit of whom the early disciples spoke was always the Spirit *of Jesus*—and Jesus had walked the stony earth, and suffered under Pontius Pilate, and endured the Cross

[1] I. John i. 1-3.   [2] *Man in Revolt*, 494.

and despised the shame. As P. T. Forsyth expressed it, "Our real and destined eternity goes
round by Nazareth to reach us." [1] "No man hath
seen God at any time; the only begotten Son, which
is in the bosom of the Father, He hath declared
Him." [2] This statement, declares Brunner, "which
would make every good Platonist's hair stand on
end, is the central article in the Christian theory of
knowledge." [3] The facts of the *kerygma* were
historic facts.

Thus by its very genesis and nature Christian
faith is inextricably involved in history. If it tries
to evade the consequences of that involvement, it
ceases to be Christian. The doctrine of the Incarnation means that God has come right into the midst
of the tumult and the shouting of this world. In
the most literal sense, it was a "down to earth"
realism that gave the Gospel birth. Therefore to
separate Christianity from social concern is to
corrupt it at its roots: in the strong language of the
apostle, it is to "make God a liar." When Jesus was
born of Mary in the stable at Bethlehem, when He
toiled at a carpenter's bench in Nazareth, when He
walked the crowded ways and lovingly identified
Himself with the struggles and the miseries of men,
when He suffered under Pontius Pilate, it was a
declaration that divine eternal truth and the tough
concrete actualities of the human situation belong
together; and "what God hath joined together let
not man put asunder." It is an unholy divorce those

---

[1] *Positive Preaching and the Modern Mind,* 18.
[2] John i. 18.   [3] *Man in Revolt,* 49.

Christians are aiding and abetting who separate
"spiritual" religion from such "material" issues as
feeding the hungry, rescuing the refugee, and en-
franchizing the racially disinherited. To prophesy
smooth things, to preach a comfortable innocuous
Gospel that leaves the crying injustices of life
untouched, is a denial of Christ every whit as
flagrant as Peter's "I know not the Man." "Blessed
is he," said Jesus, "who shall not be scandalized in
Me." [1] It is a fact we have to reckon with that there
are still thousands — and alas, not outside the
Churches only—to whom the notion that religion
might intrude into secular concerns and interfere
with economic, political and national traditions is
indeed a scandal and an offence, a thing not to be
tolerated. Hence the pathetic spectacle of preachers
and Churches eliminating the scandal by culti-
vating inoffensiveness—and losing the living Christ
in the process. This generation recognizes the
futility of a social Gospel which is merely social.
That is doomed. But do not let us twist Christ's
saying "My kingdom is not of this world" [2] into a
justification of the piety which removes politics and
economics and the way men live in the world out of
the orbit of religious concern, and imagines that by
this attitude it does God service. It does service to
no one except to the powers of darkness, whose
favourite device it is to promote by every possible
means the divorce between faith and history. What
a travesty of the truth it is when a sentimental
irrelevant quietism, trailing clouds of traditional

[1] Matt. xi. 6.   [2] John xviii. 36.

verbiage, becomes the mark of a religion professing allegiance to One who for love of men came down into the fearful pit of history and into the miry clay of the sins and miseries of all the world!

Very memorable in this connection are these words of Jacques Ellul: "When we have really understood the actual plight of our contemporaries, when we have heard their cry of anguish, and when we have understood why they won't have anything to do with our 'disembodied' Gospel, when we have shared their sufferings, both physical and spiritual, in their despair and their desolation, when we have become one with the people of our own nation and of the universal Church, as Moses and Jeremiah were one with their own people, as Jesus identified Himself with the wandering crowds, 'sheep without a shepherd,' *then* we shall be able to proclaim the Word of God—but not till then!" [1]

III

Once and For All

The facts of the *kerygma*, then, were historic facts. But they were more. For facts of history are apt to be cyclic, reappearing in the time process and repeating themselves: so that always, even of the great evolutionary climaxes of history, the question is "Look we for another?" In such rhythmical process there is nothing to bring the human mind sharply to a point. "*Iacta est alea*—yes," exclaims Brunner, "but the die will still be cast many a time,

[1] *The Presence of the Kingdom*, 141.

long after the departure of Caesar from the scene." [1]
But the facts of the Christian message were not just
historic: they were *unique*, unrepeatable, absolute,
final like the judgment trumpet, as indeed in a sense
they *were* the judgment trumpet. That is why one
of the great uncompromising notes of the New
Testament is the Greek word ἅπαξ, once and for
all. This uniqueness of the particular event, the
very conception with which mysticism and pantheism
will have nothing to do, as being alien to their ideas
of true spirituality—this very offence which to Greek
speculative thought is "foolishness"—Christianity
enthrones and makes its glory. "In that He died,"
says Paul, "He died to sin once for all." [2] "Christ
hath suffered for sins," writes Peter, "the just for
the unjust, once for all." [3] "The faith," says
Jude, "was once for all delivered to the saints." [4]
"He needeth not," declares Hebrews, "offer up
sacrifice daily, as the high priests, for this He did
once and for all, when He offered up Himself." [5]
"Once for all at the end of the world hath He
appeared, to put away sin by the sacrifice of Himself." [6] "We are sanctified through the offering of
the body of Christ once for all." [7] Even the greatest
prophets of Israel's past had no such definite claim
to make for the revelations they had brought: the
voice of prophecy rose and fell from age to age, and
died and was renewed. As the writer to the Hebrews
puts it in the two resounding adverbs with which he

---

[1] *Man in Revolt*, 442.   [2] Rom. vi. 10.   [3] I. Peter iii. 18.
[4] Jude 3.   [5] Heb. vii. 27.
[6] Heb. ix. 26, cf. ix. 12, ix. 28.   [7] Heb. x. 10.

opens his book, all previous words from the beyond had been given πολυμερῶς καὶ πολυτρόπως: they were fragmentary and disparate. But this was different. "Jesus," cries Paul, "being raised from the dead, dieth no more":[1] it happened once—never again—once and for all. The whole Bible indeed is nothing but an exposition of the uniqueness of the events by which the human situation has been decisively transformed and a new relationship between God and man established for ever. In Christ, crucified and risen, the unique divine event has happened; the final truth of God has been written into history, and the absolute has been given in terms of time. "I am not sure," said Arthur Koestler in a deeply moving and significant confession, "whether what the philosophers call 'ethical absolutes' exist, but I am sure that we have to act as if they existed."[2] There is one way in which that noble yearning of spirit can come to be sure of the absolute and know that its wistful dreams of truth and pity and compassion are in fact on the throne at the right hand of power: and that is to see the absolute written by the finger of God into history in one final unrepeatable event—in other words, to open its eyes upon Christ.

IV

THE HOUR COMETH—AND NOW IS

We have seen that the facts enshrined in the *kerygma* were historic and unique. This leads to a

[1] Rom. vi. 9.   [2] *The Listener*, 21st March 1946.

third characterization: they were *eschatological* facts.
The Day of the Lord, towards which all the prophets
had steadfastly set their faces—

> Still nursing the unconquerable hope,
> Still clutching the inviolable shade—

this, declared the early preachers, had now arrived.
The time was fulfilled. The *eschaton* had appeared.
The age of the Messiah had begun. "This," proclaimed Peter on the day of Pentecost, "is that which
was spoken by the prophet." [1] This *is* that: we are
living in it. The Kingdom of God had broken through
visibly from the beyond into the realm of the here
and now. "He has rescued us from the darkness,"
cries Paul, "and transferred us into the kingdom of
the Son of His love." [2] Men were tasting, according
to the writer to the Hebrews, "the powers of the
world to come." [3] What prophecy and apocalyptic
had spoken of as the Age to Come was present fact.

This is not to say that no place was now left for
the Advent hope and the dream of a final consummation. Once and for all, God had spoken in
history; yet history was rent with bewildering con-
tradictions. Once and for all, to use Cullmann's
figure, the decisive battle with the powers of evil had
been fought and won; yet the long campaign con-
tinued, and the final Victory Day had not come in
sight.[4] Once and for all, the Church had found the
treasure; yet it was still an earthen vessel that contained it. Once and for all, the Christian as a
redeemed man reconciled to God had passed out of

---

[1] Acts ii. 16. [2] Col. i. 13.
[3] Heb. vi. 5. [4] *Christ and Time*, 84.

death into life; yet he was still in the body, hampered by his own frailty and involved in the burden-bearing of humanity. Once and for all, heaven had stooped down to earth; yet man was a stranger and a pilgrim still. In Brunner's expressive words: "The knight has been dubbed knight, his patent of nobility has been issued, but the knight is still, in his condition, a 'commoner,' his nobility has not yet permeated his whole nature." [1] This tension pervades the New Testament; and it is bad theology which would try to resolve or eliminate it by obscuring either element —the present fulfilment or the future hope. "Christianity," declares Principal John Baillie, "must always maintain a realized and a futurist eschatology in balance, if never in equipoise." [2]

But our main concern at the moment is different. It is to see how radically apostolic preaching transcends the highest limits of prophetism. In Christ, the Messianic era had arrived. The powers of the new age were breaking through visibly into history. As Paul put it to the Corinthians: "The divine 'yes' has at last sounded in Him, for in Him is the 'yes' that affirms all the promises of God." [3]

The Gospel narratives plainly reveal this eschatological setting. Thus the mighty works of Jesus, the σημεῖα, point away beyond themselves. "The blind see, the lame walk, the lepers are cleansed, the deaf hear, the dead are raised up, to the poor the gospel is preached" [4]—these wonders, the characteristic marks of the "end time," had begun to

---

[1] *Man in Revolt*, 491.   [2] *The Belief in Progress*, 207.
[3] II. Cor. i. 20 (Moffatt).   [4] Matt. xi. 5.

happen. That it is good to perform deeds of healing and mercy was no more than every decent Jew knew already; but that in these particular works the very empire of evil was being raided and destroyed—this was something to make the morning stars sing together and the sons of God shout for joy. And it was this—nothing less—that was happening, as Jesus Himself asserted from the first, and as the disciples came to see. Every sick sufferer who was healed, every demoniac restored to sanity, every sin-rotted soul made clean was one more evidence—of what? Not simply of the emergence in Galilee of One whose power matched His pity and whose pity matched His power. That was not the significance of the events which began to be rumoured in the streets of Nazareth and Capernaum, but this—"The Lord hath made bare His holy arm in the eyes of all the nations." [1] The consummation which kings and prophets had longed in vain to see was now accomplished; and compared with this, all the prodigious forces of history, the Pharaohs and Sennacheribs and Caesars who age after age had obsessed men's minds and filled their thoughts, were trivial and puny and pathetic: "Say unto the cities of Judah, Behold your God!" [2]

It is necessary to point out that this eschatological emphasis of the apostolic preaching was not an afterthought imposed upon the facts by the Christian community: it goes back to Jesus Himself. There is a sceptical wing of the Form Critical school of New Testament interpretation which would eliminate

[1] Isaiah lii. 10.   [2] Isaiah xl. 9.

the Messianic-eschatological assertions of the Gospel
records as subsequent creations of the apocalyptic
imagination of early Christianity, *Gemeindetheologie*,
and would de-supernaturalize the Gospel picture of
Christ by explaining every passage where a divine
self-consciousness emerges as due to the retroactive
work of the Church. Hence there have been written
whole volumes about Christian origins, without one
spark in them from that conflagration which early
Christianity essentially was: a truly astonishing
accomplishment. Not in such reconstructions do
we recognize the lineaments of our holy faith: the
figure they present to us is a disembodied ghost, not
the Lord we worship and adore. But do not let us
be intimidated. This type of advanced scholarship
turns out, on closer examination, to be neither so
advanced nor so scholarly as it claims. In point of
fact, so far is it from being "advanced" that it is
quite lamentably behind the times, both critically
and theologically, and has indeed been obsolescent
these fifty years. Surely we ought by now to have
left behind the negativism of the old century-long
debate which preceded Harnack's *Das Wesen des
Christentums* in 1900! Surely we should have seen
the last of the tedious scepticism which suggests that
Jesus did not actually believe and teach about Himself what the apostles believed and taught about
Him. The evidence is there, not in one strand of
the Gospel tradition only, but in all—in Mark, in
"Q," and in the special sources drawn upon by
Matthew and Luke. It was emphatically not a case
of the community creating the supernatural tradition,

the Church producing the faith it lives by: the truth is the exact reverse. It was a case of the super- natural facts creating the community, and doing it with such irresistible momentum that to this day the gates of Hell have not prevailed against it. If the community believed Jesus to be not just another historic mode or development of revelation but actually the living truth and the ultimate apocalypse, it was because Jesus Himself had claimed it first. "If I with the finger of God cast out demons, then the Kingdom of God is come." [1] "This," He told His disciples, "is the fulfilment, the *eschaton*, which all the generations from the foundation of the world have been awaiting. You alone have seen it. Blessed are your eyes! You are the envy of the ages." [2]

Thus the apostolic preaching, which summoned men to behold God's glory in the past, and to await it in the future at the great Parousia, summoned them also to realize God's glory in the present moment. "It is the *present* Lordship of Christ, inaugurated by His resurrection and exaltation to the right hand of God, that is the centre of the faith of primitive Christianity." [3] "The hour cometh, *and now is*." [4] This was the battle-cry with which the Church faced the world. It reappears in various forms—in the primitive declaration that the Mes- sianic age has dawned, in the Pauline doctrine of life in the Spirit, in the Johannine conception of eternal life here and now, in the vivid picture in the Epistle

[1] Luke xi. 20.   [2] Matt. xiii. 16, 17.
[3] Cullmann, *The Earliest Christian Confessions*, 58.
[4] John iv. 23, v. 25.

to the Hebrews of the intersection of two worlds and of the "anchoring" of the Church to the world unseen. In short, the Church recognized itself to be a new eschatological humanity. Here, in literal fact, the human race had renewed its youth like the eagle's.

Martin Buber has said that for ourselves to-day, who live in an age when the pattern of culture and civilization is being dissolved before our eyes, the great thing is to hear rising above the abyss of our monstrous problems the wing-beat of the Spirit and the creative word. In an even deeper and more factual sense than Buber conceived, this was precisely the experience of the apostles. For them the atmosphere was charged with the supernatural: the wing-beat of the Spirit was everywhere. "If ye then are risen with Christ," writes Paul [1]—not "shall rise," but "are risen." For although the welter of the great uproarious commercial cities of Asia still remained their immediate environment, the new heaven and the new earth of apocalyptic dream had now broken in; the eschatological hope was present fact; and the Church was vibrating, as Paul told the Ephesians, with the identical power which God had exerted in taking Christ out of the grave.[2]

V

THE CONTENT OF OUR MESSAGE

We have been looking back to the preaching of the first Christian generation as it emerges from the pages of the New Testament. With this in mind,

---

[1] Col. iii. 1.   [2] Eph. i. 19-20.

we turn now to the crisis of the Church's evangelism
at the present time.   It cannot be too emphatically
stated that if contemporary evangelism is to make its
full potential impact on the secularism of this age,
it will have to go back more constantly and deliberately than it has done, and also more patiently
and humbly, to its own fountain-head in the New
Testament, and test there its message to this generation, re-examining in that light the content, the
claim, and the communication of its message.   Consider these three aspects of the matter.

First, as to *the content of the message* to the modern
world.   We have seen that the apostolic *kerygma*
dealt, not in religious ideas, but in facts: it spoke
not of spiritual theories, but of events—historic,
unique, eschatological events.   Now if we accept
this as our standard, we must realize it is not sufficient to offer men and women a set of what we may
call "Christian ideas," in the hope that they may be
prevailed upon to appropriate and assimilate these,
and eventually work them into the patterns of
civilization and the texture of society.   No amount
of assimilation of religious ideas, even if they are the
best and noblest, will ever constitute a man a
Christian or reveal to a secular culture the glory of
the Kingdom of God.   In any case, the unspoken
cry of every gathered congregation to the preacher
is not "Is there any bright idea from the current
religious debate?" but "Is there any word from the
Lord?"—not "We would see what advice may be
available," but "We would see Jesus."   Karl Barth
was not using words loosely or unadvisedly when he

said, describing a congregation gathering for worship, "The situation on Sunday morning is eschatological. The ultimate desire of man, the desire for
an ultimate event, now becomes authoritative." [1]
Christianity means devotion to the Person of Christ,
incarnate, crucified, risen. And evangelism means
to-day just what it meant at the first: opening men's
lives to the impact of historic, unique, eschatological
events, events which—just because they are eschatological—are indeed truly present whenever they are
truly proclaimed, and because they are present,
implacably demand decision.

How urgent this task now is may be illustrated
from a remark made in a recent discussion on Bible
instruction in the schools: "Let us teach them the
ideas of the Fatherhood of God and the brotherhood
of man—but that is all: the Christian rudiments—
none of your supernatural accretions, none of your
sectarian theology." An alarming revelation surely
of the confusion that can exist even in Christian
minds! What right have we—for the sake of an
educational syllabus, or for anything else—to define
Christianity in terms which implicitly deny the
presuppositions of every sentence the men of the
New Testament wrote? The fact, of course, is that
what this speaker wished to ban as sectarian theology
was—had he only allowed himself to see it staring
at him from every page of the Gospels and Acts
and Epistles—no subsequent sectarian accretion to
Christian doctrine, but the original and basic
essence of the faith.

[1] *The Word of God and the Word of Man,* 110.

In any case this attitude is symptomatic of confused and muddled thinking. It holds to the idea of the Fatherhood of God as being more liberal and easier of acceptance than the historical basis of Christian orthodoxy, and as being a convenient escape from the radical supernaturalism of the Christian claim: not realizing apparently that the belief in the existence of a living, personal Father God is the most supernatural belief of all. That by the way.

The fact remains that the greatest drag on Christianity to-day, the most serious menace to the Church's mission, is not the secularism without, it is the reduced Christianity within: the religious generalities and innocuous platitudes of a pallid, anaemic Christianity which is simply (in the language of arithmeticians) the "highest common factor" of half a dozen different religions. This is what Kierkegaard called "a vaporized Christianity, a culture consciousness, the dregs of Christianity." [1] Dr. John Mackay's warning is timely: "The Christian Church, were it to admit syncretism as a religious ideal, would lose any compelling sense of missionary obligation." [2] No doubt this substitute faith, this modern version of ancient theosophical syncretism, this "Christianity made easy," represents often a sincere and in its own way laudable attempt to construct a bridge between modern culture and the New Testament faith, between the scientific-critical spirit of the age and historic

[1] *The Journals of Sören Kierkegaard*, translated and edited by Alexander Dru, 437.

[2] *Theology To-day*, Jan. 1951, p. 433.

Christianity. Did not Paul himself say, "I am become all things to all men, that I might by all means save some"? [1] Yes, indeed: but not at the self-defeating cost of changing Christianity into something else, not at the cost of soft-pedalling the historical-supernatural elements without which Christianity does not exist, or of dissolving the divine intolerance of the faith in a morass of religious relativism. "So long as the modern New Testament reader is consciously or unconsciously interpreting it in terms of a humanitarian ethic or of a humanitarian spiritual experience, he is sinning against the meaning of words." [2] This religion of a Jesus who taught wonderful philosophical truths about nature and providence and held views on politics in advance of His time, this pantheistic worship of a God who "does everything in general and nothing in particular," [3] is a poor and watery substitute for the strong and vital faith of the apostles in One who was greater than the prophets, greater than the Lord's Anointed, greater than Messiah, invading time from the beyond, and cleaving history asunder with the shattering words, "Before Abraham was, I am!" [4]

"At every period in the history of the Church," writes Emil Brunner, "the greatest sin of the Church, and the one which causes the greatest distress, is that she withholds the Gospel from the world and from herself. Whether the corruption of the message be

---

[1] I. Cor. ix. 22.
[2] Hoskyns and Davey, *The Riddle of the New Testament*, 33.
[3] Leonard Hodgson, *The Doctrine of the Atonement*, 122.
[4] John viii. 58.

the orthodox form which does not distinguish between human doctrine and the Divine Word of God,
and therefore preaches the creed of yesterday instead
of the living Word; or the Pietist error which
diverts interest from the Word and the Promise of
God to the individual and his subjective experiences
and feelings; or the Liberal and Rationalistic error
which confuses the Word of God with reason, and
instead of the message of the Cross offers a religious
ethic or a mystical asceticism: in principle it all
comes to the same thing in the end, because each
error is akin to all the others. . . . The weakness of
the Church lies in the fact that she lacks this 'Living
Word'—that she does not know the reason for her
own existence—and consequently has no real message
for the present situation."[1]

Is it not time we insisted that the heretical
Christology of a reduced Gospel is not only religiously indefensible but even critically unsound?
It is bad scholarship, to put it no higher. It represents an arbitrary and quite unscientific juggling
with facts, to suit its own presuppositions. "If you
believe what you like in the Gospel," said Augustine,
"and reject what you like, it is not the Gospel you
believe, but yourselves." For example, I am at
liberty to take out of the Gospels Jesus the social
reformer. But I am simply blinding my eyes if I
do not take simultaneously the fact of the unique
communion with God, the secret life of prayer, from
which that social passion sprang. I may take Jesus
the teacher of a new revolutionary ethic. But I have

[1] *The Divine Imperative*, 565.

no right to do that if I am going to neglect the
revolutionary self-consciousness behind every word
in which that ethic was presented. I may take
Jesus the Redeemer of the natural and the Lord of
human nature: but I am deceiving myself, I am
playing fast and loose with the records and indulging
in a piece of purely artificial selection, if I leave out
the supernatural claim on which that Lordship rests.
Such treatment of the Gospel narrative is—even from
the standpoint of accurate exegesis—vulnerable and
illogical and unsound. Religiously, it is disastrous.
It is truly astonishing that so many of our latter-day
prophets can go on punctually producing their
revised versions of the Christian faith, without even
noticing that these polished novelties of theirs are
just the same old mildewed heresies which the
ancient Church exploded eighteen hundred years ago!

If evangelism is to make any impression on the
modern world, it must at all costs resist the sterilizing
and paralysing influence of such reductions of the
historic faith. It must still assert, as did the original
kerygma, that in Christ the new age has arrived. It
must still proclaim that the history of man is not
just a level horizontal process from the past into the
future, with Utopia or the Kingdom of Heaven
somewhere away at the end; for in Christ the present
moment is charged with the transcendental, and the
Kingdom of Heaven is here. It must still insist that
men can be sons of God, can pass, that is, from the
level of their ordinary biological human existence
into life of a new dimension, from βίος to ζωή—in
Johannine language, from being "born of the flesh"

to being "born of the Spirit";[1] not indeed by climbing up from the one level to the other by their own efforts or by some form of emergent evolution, but precisely because in Christ the new dimension, the supernatural quality of life, has reached down to them; because (to vary the figure) just as the vine injects its life into the branch, so Christ imparts to those who receive Him the very life of God.[2]

In short, it must not shrink from the ultimate alternatives. Either, in Christ, God the Creator and Redeemer came right into human life, or else the Gospels are the record of a lie. Either the Pauline experience of being risen with Christ is the most stupendous and practical of all realities, or else the whole make-up of our religion is sophistry and sham. Either this present generation can be baptized into the very life of God, or else Jesus spoke falsely. I can understand a man, with the faith in front of him, saying "That's true! It is the very key to life, and the one thing worth proclaiming." I can almost understand a man saying "It can't be true! I refuse to touch it." What I simply cannot understand is a man saying "Yes, it is true, it exists to be proclaimed; but I will take out of it only the insights and beliefs it shares in common with other religions, and leave the rest." Not so did Christianity go out at the first to meet the paganisms and half-beliefs, the conflicting philosophies and multiform mythologies of Hellenistic culture. It is only by being true to its origins and by declaring the full apostolic content of the message that evangelism can achieve

[1] John iii. 6.   [2] John xv. 1 ff.

its characteristic work and convince the world that in Christ is life, and the life is the light of men.[1]

How challenging to the preacher in this connection become these words from Kierkegaard's *Journals*: "There is something quite definite I have to say, and I have it so much upon my conscience that (as I feel) I dare not die without having uttered it. For the instant I die and thus leave this world (so I understand it) I shall in the very same second be infinitely far away, in a different place where still within the same second the question will be put to me: 'Hast thou uttered the definite message *quite definitely?*' And if I have not done so, what then?" [2]

VI

The Claim of God

I pass from the content of the message to *its claim*. In the New Testament, the *kerygma* claims authority in and for itself. That is to say, the Gospel preached by the apostles was not a means to an end. It was not offered, for example, as a social-political lever. Men were asked to accept it for its own sake. Being based on unique, final, absolute facts, it had an absolute claim. It was not an instrument for some other object regarded as more ultimate and more important. It was God's life manifested and offered. It *was*, from the foundation of the world. It would see history out at last. It stood in its own right. This was the claim.

[1] John i. 4.   [2] *Journals* (ed. Dru), 493.

To-day the emphasis is different. I wonder if we are aware how widespread is the tendency, even amongst Christian people, to regard the faith as a means to an end, and how often evangelism comes to be tinged with this disquieting colour. I am not thinking of blatant instances, such as that of the high-ranking officer who argued for Army Chaplaincies on the ground that they increased the morale of the troops (which, while perfectly true, was so remote from the Christian understanding of the matter that the late Archbishop Temple in point of fact characterized it as sheer blasphemy); nor the other instance of a certain distinguished Church member who contributed liberally to foreign missions as being a stabilizing factor in the structure of the British Commonwealth. Incidentally, this view of missions was only partially valid; the contributor in question had probably failed to realize that the missionary proclamation of the Word of God is a dynamic and disturbing force which sometimes will produce not political and economic stabilization but revolution. Communism is not the only breaker of the peace in lands like Africa to-day. "I am come," said Jesus, "to send fire on the earth," [1] and there are fields where the Christian mission has done precisely that: agelong complacent traditions of caste and serfdom and racial inferiority have begun to go down like stubble before the devouring flame. But in any case it is not of glaring instances of ulterior motive such as those I have mentioned that I am thinking now, but of the familiar type of

[1] Luke xii. 49.

argument which says, for example—"We are living
in an age when liberty is being encroached upon and
filched away. Religion is the buttress of true liberty.
Therefore let us recall men to religion." Or again—
"We want a new order of society. The best lever
for social regeneration is religion. Therefore let us
present religion as the surest hope of the fulfilment
of legitimate social aspirations." Or again—"Civilization with its new-found powers of destruction is
doomed, unless men learn to live as brothers. Christ
holds the secret of true brotherhood and the renewal
of civilization. Therefore let us preach Christ."
Now notice, in each case, the premises of the argument are strictly accurate. That is why anyone who
raises a question about the validity of this type of
argument is liable to be misunderstood. Religion *is*,
in point of fact, the true buttress of liberty and
democracy. It *is* the best lever for social reform.
Once and again in history, as Toynbee points out,
Christianity has bridged the gap between the dis-
integrating of one form of civilization and the birth
of another.[1] There is no other force in existence
which can do so much along these lines as Christianity. The premises are true, and the Church
needs to stress them more, not less; for too often
in the past the Church has failed conspicuously to
realize its involvement in the historic situation, and
has been culpably apathetic towards social, economic
and international ideals: a failure for which it has
set itself energetically to make amends to-day. Now
all this makes the very suggestion of the question I

[1] *Christianity and Civilisation,* 15.

am raising liable to misconstruction. But the risk
has to be taken. Let me put the point quite simply.
I wonder whether sometimes, when our evangelism
fails, the reason may not be that we have been
refusing to let Christ shine in His own light. It is
true, as I have said, that the Incarnation is social
dynamite; it is true that the Cross is the mightiest
lever for lifting the world above the reach of the
forces of destruction. But thus to present the faith
as a means to an end—even if it be a noble end—is
sooner or later to make the Cross of Christ of none
effect: yes, and of none effect even as the social
lever it has the power to be.

Some words of Herbert Butterfield in his book
Christianity and History are worth pondering in this
connection. "If I say that I see nothing which is
likely to touch the present situation of the world
except Christianity, I do not mean that it is the
function of religion to save civilization or that
Christianity is a thing to which we resort to rescue a
system and order that are either decrepit or under
the judgment of Heaven. One could not say that
such a faith is properly appropriated when it is
adopted with the object of getting society out of a
scrape." [1]

Take an analogy. Not long ago one of our
leading scientists expressed the belief that in this
atomic age sheer expediency would teach men ethics.
"Science," he declared, "is going to make us behave
better, or else to kill us. We have got to behave
better than our forefathers, because we live in a

[1] P. 130.

world where the consequences of collective wrong-
doing are much more dangerous." Of course the
argument was nonsense, but he did not seem to see
the double fallacy: on the one hand, that life does
not work out like that, and the prospect of danger
does not in fact produce morality; and on the other
hand, that if it did, what was produced would not
be moral, for morality consists in doing what is right
for its own sake, because it is right; and to ask the
question "Why be moral?"—thus making morality
a means to an end—is itself an immoral proceeding.

This holds good even more emphatically for
religion. The apostolic *kerygma* was right: the
Gospel is to be offered for its own sake, which means
for Christ's sake. This is the claim. God is not a
force to be used, not even to advance the purposes
of civilization. No doubt it is true that God will not
stop to inquire into motives when a nation in peril
of its existence or a whole recalcitrant generation
returns to Him at last, any more than He inquires
into the motives of one lost soul limping home from
the far country. Even if the motive is mainly self-
preservation—"How many have bread enough and
to spare, and I perish with hunger!" [1]—this is
sufficient. After all it was Jephthah, not Jehovah,
who said, "Why are you come unto me now when
you are in distress?" [2] The word of the Lord is:
"Him that cometh I will in no wise cast out." [3]
Nevertheless, not by making it a means to an end
do we commend the faith once for all delivered to
the saints. Here is a religion that has an absolute

[1] Luke xv. 17.   [2] Judges xi. 7.   [3] John vi. 37.

claim. The coming of atomic energy and astro-physics has not modified that claim by one iota, nor shaken its totalitarian demand. The *kerygma* stands in its own right. We accept and we preach the Gospel for its own sake, knowing that here the living God confronts men and nations and cultures in judgment and in mercy, and offers to them through Christ His own eternal life.

VII

THE COMMUNICATION OF THE WORD

I pass finally to *the communication of the message.* For even when its content and its claim are clear, the problem remains: how is it to be brought home to men and women of this generation? How is it to be communicated? The major difficulty, as every conference on evangelism almost monotonously reiterates, is just this difficulty of communication. How are we to make the great Christian words— grace, salvation, justification, faith—intelligible, how are we to make the message compulsive, for an age and a culture largely de-christianized by the cor-roding acids of a ubiquitous secularism? Has the apostolic preaching anything to teach us here? I believe it has—something which deserves fuller attention than it has yet received.

Let me put it in a sentence. In the apostolic age, *the very act of proclaiming the good news was caught up into the context of the truth proclaimed and itself became part of the Gospel.* I mean that those men, risen with

Christ, were themselves part of the message of the
Resurrection. The Church for which they spoke,
being Christ's Body, was itself part of the Incarnation. Their theme, as we have found, concerned
events in which God had visibly confronted the
human race; but as they preached these events, in
that same moment and by that very act God was
confronting men again. In short, the proclamation
of the mighty acts of God's redemption was itself
a continuance of the divine redeeming activity.
Praedicatio verbi divini est verbum divinum.[1]

There is a point here which has too often been
overlooked. No doubt the Greek word *kerygma*, as
used in the New Testament, signifies the thing proclaimed rather than the act of proclaiming. But to
draw this distinction too rigidly would be misleading:
it would blur the vitally important fact that in the
New Testament the act of proclaiming the message
always becomes part of the message proclaimed.
When Paul preached to Felix "the faith in Christ"
and "reasoned of judgment,"[2] something more than
that was happening. God was there and then
judging the man by that confrontation with the
living Christ. "This is the judgment, that light is
come."[3] In the same way, the announcement of
God's redeeming activity was itself God in action to
redeem. The Gospel existed and lived, not in
documentary evidence and doctrinal formulae, but
only in being proclaimed. Preaching, as P. T.
Forsyth maintained, is far more than the declaration
of a Gospel. "It is the Gospel prolonging and

---

[1] Bullinger. [2] Acts xxiv. 24, 25. [3] John iii. 19.

declaring itself." [1] Suppose the first Christians had
said, "God has invaded history in power and great
glory: that is sufficient. We can leave the facts to
make their own way in the world"—the Gospel
would have been stultified. No Christians would
have been made. But they went out and proclaimed
the facts, and the very proclamation constituted for
the hearers a divine invasion crisis. Even as they
listened, Christ was coming again to be their Judge
and their Redeemer. "The hour cometh—and now
is." Just as every celebration of the Sacrament was
literally, as Paul observed, "a showing forth of the
Lord's death," [2] just as the corporate life of the
Church was Christ's daily renewed self-disclosure in
the power of His Resurrection, so the preaching of
the word was in actual fact the living personal Word
breaking in from the beyond, taking charge of the
situation and going creatively to work. In short, every
such act of the apostles was quite literally an act
of God.

If this is indeed the inner meaning of Christian
preaching, if the proclamation of the Word belongs itself to *Heilsgeschichte* as an integral part of
God's continuous saving activity, how immeasurably
significant becomes the vocation of the preacher!
And how tragically we blunder if for any reason
whatever we disparage it or think meanly of this
chosen way by which the living Christ still purposes
to go forth to save!

But to return to the problem of the communication

---

[1] *Positive Preaching and the Modern Mind,* 3.
[2] I. Cor. xi. 26.

of the message to-day. It ought now to be clear
that the problem is not to be solved merely or
mainly, as some suggest, by a retranslation of
archaic religious terminology into the current
language of the hour. This has its place, of course.
"As the Bible had to be translated by the missionary
Church into the most widely differing languages,
and as this translation work has been, and still is,
one of the most important achievements of the
Mission of the Church, so the Gospel has to be
continually retranslated into contemporary terms—
a task which the Church ought to take far more
seriously than she has done of late." [1] Yet I suspect
that much of the talk one hears about the incom-
prehensibleness of the vocabulary of religion to the
man in the street is extravagance, to say nothing of
its being a slur upon the average man's intelligence.
But in any case the nerve of the problem is not there.
For *kerygma* is so much more than the recounting of
certain facts, whether this be done in Aramaic or
Hellenistic Greek or Basic English or anything else;
and all theological reinterpretation and all evangelism
will be only "words, words, words" unless they are
the Creative Word. Peter could have told on the
streets of Jerusalem the facts about Christ, could
have kept on recounting the events of the Gospel,
without doing anything that could remotely be described by the verb the New Testament uses for
"preach." "A 'sound film' of the life of Jesus
taken by a neutral reporter," writes Brunner, "or an
account of the life of Jesus written by an unbelieving

[1] Brunner, *The Christian Doctrine of God*, Dogmatics, I. 68.

compiler—such as Josephus, for instance—would not have the power to awaken faith in Jesus." [1] Christian preaching begins only when faith in the message has reached such a pitch that the man or the community proclaiming it becomes part of the message proclaimed. "These Christians must show me they are redeemed," cried Nietzsche, "before I will believe in their Redeemer." Thus when the apostolic Church declared, "The hour cometh, and now is: this is the age of the Spirit," the Church itself in its total life was part of that dramatic truth; for men encountering that Church felt, even though they were pagans, a waft of the supernatural, a mysterious power like the stirring of a dawn wind. Hence Professor T. W. Manson's aphorism is strictly accurate: "The doctrine of the Church is a branch of Christology." [2] In the words of the unknown second-century writer of the letter to Diognetus, "What the soul is in the body, this the Christians are in the world." [3] The Spirit of Christ has always been His own best evidence.

In the last resort, therefore, the problem of communication resolves itself into a question of faith: faith in the message, the kind of faith which, being *fiducia* and not mere *assensus*, is an act uniting the messenger to the Christ of whom his message tells— so that every time the message is told, the whole situation is charged with the supernatural, the whole redeeming energy of the eternal is concentrated, Christ Himself is veritably at work, and the Cross

---

[1] *Op. cit.* 36.   [2] *The Church's Ministry,* 20.
[3] ὅπερ ἐστὶν ἐν σώματι ψυχή, τοῦτ᾽ εἰσὶν ἐν κόσμῳ Χριστιανοί.

and the Resurrection are no longer past events but present realities in which the living God meets men and challenges them to decision. "From faith to faith" is the apostolic characterization of the Gospel message: [1] for faith first unites to Christ, and then Christ the Creative Word, being thus present, arouses faith beyond and brings in His new creation. The exalted Lord who first made Himself known to Peter and John and Paul uses the testimony of their faith, and through that testimony gives Himself to a thousand others. This was the Church's hidden secret. For just as religion is never merely a theological debate but always worship and obedience, so apostolic Christianity is never merely familiarity with the facts, but always union with the risen Christ. And what we *ought* to mean when we talk about "the unity of the New Testament" is something deeper than a common proclamation or body of beliefs distinguishable through all its diverse parts: the real unity of the New Testament is the unity of life, a life flowing from the risen Christ. When Gibbon, in his *Decline and Fall*, attributed the victory of Christianity to five reasons—Christian enthusiasm, belief in immortality, miracles, ethics, and organization—he had left out the one decisive factor: [2] the presence in the proclamation of the living Christ. For what men heard, listening to the apostles, was not simply a human testimony: it was the self-testimony of the risen Jesus. They did not say, "This is the truth: we will learn it, and it will

---

[1] Rom. i. 17.
[2] *The Decline and Fall of the Roman Empire*, xv.

instruct us." They said, "This is the Lord: we have waited for Him, and He will save us."

"There is ultimately only one religious difficulty," James Denney used to say, "the difficulty of being religious." So now we may also add: there is ultimately only one problem of communication of the Christian message—the problem of allowing myself, yourself, as the messengers, to be taken command of by the risen Christ.

For the crux of all evangelism still lies in that one dramatic paradox, which some scholars disparage and discount as unpractical mysticism and apostolic rhetoric, but which in point of fact is vibrant with the most practical and decisive force in all the world: "I, yet not I, but Christ." [1]

To be thus taken command of, so that our testimony, when we go out to speak of Christ, is not ours at all, but Christ's self-testimony—this is our vocation and the hope of our ministry. It is God's great promise and demand to every preacher of the Word. Here, in all reverence and humility, the disciple may take upon his lips the saying of his Lord: "To this end was I born, and for this cause came I into the world." [2]

---

[1] Gal. ii. 20.   [2] John xviii. 37.

CHAPTER TWO

PROCLAIMING FORGIVENESS

Wilt Thou forgive that sin where I begun,
   Which was my sin, though it were done before?
Wilt Thou forgive that sin, through which I run,
   And do run still, though still I do deplore?
      When Thou hast done, Thou hast not done,
         For I have more.

I have a sin of fear, that when I have spun
   My last thread, I shall perish on the shore;
But swear by Thyself, that at my death Thy Son
   Shall shine as He shines now, and heretofore;
      And having done that, Thou hast done,
         I fear no more.
               JOHN DONNE, *Hymn to God the Father.*

ONE of the main difficulties about preaching is to make sure you are speaking to everyone. Some texts and subjects may fail completely to find their mark with some of the hearers; and then you have people going away from a service saying, "Well, that did not get me, at any rate!" But there is one theme which concerns all without exception: and this is the forgiveness of sins. "All we like sheep have gone astray; we have turned every one to his own way" [1]; so that when the men of Scripture speak to us of this, every one of us can say—"This means me."

Now one of the most notable characteristics of the apostolic preaching was this—that it really did convey to men the wonder of the experience of being forgiven. You must have noticed the immensely significant fact that the most lyrical outbursts of

[1] Isaiah *liii.* 6.

sudden poetry and doxology, both in the Old Testament and in the New, are those that celebrate forgiveness. "Who is a God like unto Thee?" cries Micah, challenging in the name of Jehovah of Israel all the imperial pomps of the terrible deities of the nations, "who is a God like unto Thee?"[1] But the extraordinary significance of the prophetic jubilation lies in the words which immediately follow, as giving the characteristic action of Israel's God within history and among men: not "Who is a God like unto Thee, that rideth on the wings of the wind and treadeth on the high places of the earth?"; not "Who is a God like unto Thee, that confoundeth the devices of the sinner and holdeth the wicked in derision?"; but this—"Who is a God like unto Thee, that pardoneth iniquity, and passeth by transgression, retaining not His anger for ever, because He delighteth in mercy?" This, declare the men of Scripture unanimously, is His crowning glory, this is the final amazement.

> Great God of wonders! all Thy ways
> Are worthy of Thyself—Divine;
> But the bright glories of Thy grace
> Beyond Thine other wonders shine.
> Who is a pardoning God like Thee,
> Or who has grace so rich and free?[2]

I would that something of that same jubilant exhilaration might stir within our Churches still. For it is an incomparable experience to be forgiven. We are hearing much in these days about the

---

[1] Micah vii. 18.   [2] Samuel Davies.

Church and the ministry of healing. We are being told—I for one believe quite truly—that the Church has too much neglected this part of its commission. But I submit that in this whole debate there is one fact that is too often overlooked. It is this—*that wherever the Church truly proclaims the forgiveness of sins there the healing ministry is veritably at work.* Who can tell the incalculable results of the word of absolution for the integration of human personalities? Who can say how many demons are being exorcized, how many potentialities of mental trouble, neurasthenia and even organic disease are being rooted out by the assurance of pardon and renewal? "I always send my patients," said a distinguished psychiatrist, "to hear Dr. So-and-so preach: he preaches the forgiveness of sins." "The forgiveness of God, in my opinion," writes Dr. Leslie D. Weatherhead, "is the most powerful therapeutic idea in the world." [1] Never let us doubt the immense tides of healing energy—for soul and mind and body—which may flow through every Church and every ministry that faithfully proclaim the apostolic word: "The blood of Jesus Christ His Son καθαρίζει ἡμᾶς—goes on cleansing us—from all sin." [2]

But now to return. The true profundity of the Christian conception of forgiveness and the essential splendour of the Christian experience can disclose themselves only to those who have faced and answered three fundamental, inescapable questions. In one form or another, these questions continually recur; they haunt not only the thinking of theologians,

---

[1] *Psychology, Religion and Healing*, 338.　　[2] I. John i. 7.

they haunt the agelong human struggle with temptation; they confront every new generation and every individual soul, and inexorably demand an answer. In particular, they rise, even though it be inarticulately, from every gathered congregation and thrust themselves—here wistfully, there fervently, sometimes it may be with a passionate despair—upon the man who has to speak to his fellows in the name of God. As we face these questions now, they will lead us to the very heart of the preacher's task.

I

THE ARMOUR OF AN ILLUSION

First: *Is forgiveness necessary?* Suppose this. Suppose I tell a man that the essential thing about the Christian Gospel is its offer of forgiveness. Suppose I say to him, in the words of St. Paul, "God for Christ's sake hath forgiven you." [1] Suppose that thereupon he retorts, "There is some mistake! Christ has come to the wrong address. Forgiveness? For me? What do I need it for? No doubt there are plenty of others who have blundered and made a sad mess of things—that is why the world is in such a sorry plight—but I? What have I done, that I should be forgiven? That is not troubling me!"

What would you say about this attitude? Obviously you would have to say that there was a man who did not believe in forgiveness because he did

---

[1] Eph. iv. 32.

not believe in the reality of sin. In St. Anselm's phrase, *nondum considerasti quanti ponderis sit peccatum.* Begin further back with that man. Question him about sin; and as likely as not, you will encounter the withering supercilious challenge: "Surely you are not going to raise that old bogey! Sin? The mere moonshine of an antediluvian Calvinism! And even granting the fact of human frailty, are not Abana and Pharpar better than all the waters of Israel—our native humanism better than any outmoded Jordan? Did not Spinoza in his *Ethics* announce, 'Evil is nothing positive'? Be sensible. Do you think the Power behind the universe is going to care how I choose to run my life? It has more to do. *Dieu pardonnera, c'est son métier!* God will pat the sinner on the back and say, 'There, there! You did not mean it. It does not matter!' And therefore forgiveness is not necessary. Keep it for those who want it: don't come offering it to me!"

It is important to notice that this attitude manifests itself also on the scale of communities and cultures and civilizations. It was precisely this romantic myth about human nature which underlay the Victorian gospel of inevitable progress; and it still inspires the Marxist illusion to-day. After the revolution is complete—so runs the belief—the egotism inseparable from the institutions of property and capital will be eliminated. This naïve Utopianism is just the old denial of sin's reality in a fresh guise. "No cumulation of contradictory evidence," says Reinhold Niebuhr, "seems to disturb modern

man's good opinion of himself." [1]   Kierkegaard indeed recommended the Divinity students of the
Denmark of his day to take a dose of Schopenhauer
to disinfect them against the prevalent theological
optimism which he called "that twaddle." [2]   It is
told that Frederick the Great once had to listen to a
sermon which glibly glorified the idea of progress—
man was a marvellous creature who would soon work
out his salvation and make the earth a Paradise: but
Frederick, growing impatient, looked scornfully at
that idle chatterer and muttered, *Er kennt die ver-
dammte Rasse nicht.*   Or, as it might be put, he has
forgotten the sheer devil in the human heart, the
anarchic passions of the soul.

> 'Tis the faith that launched point-blank her dart
>   At the head of a lie—taught Original Sin,
> The corruption of Man's Heart.[3]

This is the rock on which evolutionary romanticism
will always go to pieces.

But come back to the man who, minimizing sin,
denies the necessity of forgiveness.   Even he presumably has momentary twinges of disquiet and
self-accusing.   "The   bad   conscience,"   writes
Brunner, "is like a dog which is shut up in the
cellar on account of its tiresome habit of barking,
but is continually on the watch to break into the
house which is barred against him, and is able to do
so the moment the master's vigilance is relaxed.   The
bad conscience is always there, it is chronic." [4]   This

---

[1] *The Nature and Destiny of Man*, i. 100.   [2] *Journals*, 507.
[3] Robert Browning, *Gold Hair: A Story of Pornic*.   [4] *Man in Revolt*, 202.

is doubtless true. Yet men and nations and even
Churches do appear to achieve an astonishing degree
of success in repairing their damaged complacency
and silencing their uneasy conscience. Much of our
present day ecclesiastical orthodoxy is simply crypto-
pelagianism. "We have Churches," wrote P. T.
Forsyth, "of the nicest, kindest people, who have
nothing apostolic or missionary, who never knew the
soul's despair or its breathless gratitude." [1] For
once sin has been rationalized away, a doctrine of
forgiveness will always appear superfluous and
irrelevant.

II

God's Way of Piercing the Armour

This, then, is one aspect of the situation confronting the Church and the preacher of the Word.
Thus the question arises: Are there any facts which
can pierce the armour of this illusion? How shall
the preacher drive home to human hearts to-day the
judgment and the mercy of the Lord? I wish to
suggest three such facts.

First, *the chaos of the world*. *Habet mundus*, wrote
St. Bernard long ago, *noctes suas et non paucas*. Our
own age has seen one of the darkest of these nights;
and if theology has tried at times to discard the
doctrine of original sin, the historical situation itself
is to-day rewriting that doctrine deep into the uneasy
conscience of the race. What we are realizing to-day
is our corporate involvement in the human dilemma;

[1] *Positive Preaching and the Modern Mind*, 244.

the moral failure of one generation vitiates the moral insights of the next, confuses its judgment and perverts its will. Consider—to take but one illustration —the refugee problem. We may say we are not to blame that there are millions of refugees in the world, with all the dreadful detailed misery which this grim modern fact involves. But are we burdened with the fact? Has Christ's "Inasmuch" really pierced us to the heart? Has a comfortable religiosity never blunted for us the cutting edge of Christ's terrible compassion? And besides, are we so sure that in the eyes of God no blame attaches to ourselves? The fact is, we are all interlocked in one great tragic predicament of sin, frustration and corruption. "The whole world," said St. John, "lieth in the power of the Evil One." [1] Man's dilemma is cosmic—"the Kingdom of sin," of which Ritschl spoke, over against the Kingdom of God. We cannot detach ourselves from this situation: when we look upon the distortion and dislocation and devilry of the world we feel ashamed—and not only ashamed of humanity, but ashamed of ourselves. For we, too, have a share in the sinful disposition, the bias that clogs the spirit; we, too, are infected and defiled. And therefore repentance must be of the kind described by Kierkegaard when he said, "I must repent myself back into the family, into the clan, into the race, back to God." [2] No man who has honestly confronted the chaos of the world can long keep up the pretence of talking of forgiveness as unnecessary.

[1] I. John v. 19.   [2] W. Lowrie, *A Short Life of Kierkegaard*, 101.

The second fact which pierces the armour of that illusion is *the character of Christ*. Here we impinge upon one of the most important of current theological debates. There are certain types of modern theology which express themselves as indifferent to the character of Christ. Reacting violently against the concentration on "the Jesus of History," which marked the liberal evangelicalism of a former generation, they now tell us that it is a misdirection of theological interest to focus any attention at all on the life and person of the historic Jesus; that in any case that life was not a revelation but a veiling of God; and that what matters is not the character of Christ but the dogma of the Saviour who came to earth and died and was exalted. No doubt this swing of the theological pendulum was inevitable: no doubt it was a salutary rebuke to a one-sided liberalism; but it has gone too far. Certainly it has lost the New Testament perspective. Any man who can read the New Testament Epistles—many sections, for example of St. Paul's letters, and very notably such documents as the Epistle to the Hebrews and the First Epistle of St. John—and deny that the apostolic Church was vitally concerned with the personality and lineaments of the historic Jesus and the decisive significance of His example, is simply shutting his eyes to the facts. We have all the apostolic warrant that we need for preaching the character of Christ.

This, then, is the second angle from which to meet the question, Is Forgiveness necessary? "I may not be a saint"—you know the familiar speech—

"I am not a saint, but at least I am as good as
So-and-so." How that argument shrivels up when
Jesus comes anywhere near it! "He hath a daily
beauty in his life," said Iago of Cassio in the play,
"that makes me ugly." And when we stand before
the character of Jesus, do we not feel the same?
He hath a daily beauty in His life that challenges me
daily and makes me ugly. Augustine in his earlier
years was a self-indulgent young scholar in the
University of Carthage, full of complacency and
compromise: "there sang all around me in my
ears," he declares, "a cauldron of unholy loves."
But one day Jesus crossed his path, and he was
humbled to the dust. "You took me," cried
Augustine, "from behind my own back, where I had
put myself all the time that I preferred not to see
myself. And You set me there before my face that
I might see how vile I was. . . . I saw myself and was
horrified." [1] "The Lord turned," records an evangelist, "and looked upon Peter. And Peter remem-
bered." [2] And he went out—this strong man—and
cried like a child. Thus pride is shattered by the
holiness of Christ. The autarchy of the self-
righteous man is broken down. And where is the
man who can bring his life into the white light of
the character of Jesus—that matchless nobility, that
measureless spirituality—and still think that he has
nothing to be forgiven? This is the light in which
the preacher stands, and knows himself to be less
than the least of all the saints: that God should
commission *him* of all people to such a vocation is

[1] *Confessions*, iii. 1.   [2] Luke xxii. 61.

the sheer amazement of grace abounding to the chief
of sinners. This is the light in which true preaching
places the hearers, so that in every congregation
where the Word is faithfully proclaimed the sacri-
fices of God are indeed a broken spirit and a contrite
heart. Here, in the character of Christ, is the light-
ning-flash across the midnight of man's self-deceiv-
ing. So, cries Browning, about one blinded soul—

> So may the truth be flashed out by one blow,
> And Guido see, one instant, and be saved.[1]

The third fact to destroy the illusion that forgiveness is unnecessary is the *Cross of Christ*. Dr.
Stanley Jones has told of the conversion of a man
who was a Government official in India. His work
took him away from home. He was tempted. He
fell into ways of dishonesty and shame. As time
went on, the burden of his guilt tormented him.
One day he called his wife into the room and began
unfolding the whole wretched story. As the meaning
of his words dawned on her, she turned pale as death,
staggered against the wall, and leant there with tears
on her face, as though she had been struck with a
whip. "In that moment," he said afterwards, "I saw
the meaning of the Cross. I saw love crucified by
sin." And when it was over, and she said she loved
him still and would not leave him but would help
him back to a new life, it was conversion—salvation.

As Karl Barth has put it: "Sin scorches us when
it comes under the light of forgiveness, not before.
Sin scorches us then." [2]

---

[1] *The Ring and the Book*, x.   [2] *Credo*, 45.

What the apostolic preaching did was to show men the Cross of Christ, and their own share in it; and preaching dare not do less to-day. "As a race," wrote P. T. Forsyth, "we are not even stray sheep, or wandering prodigals merely; we are rebels taken with weapons in our hands." [1] Therefore we must not leave men labouring under the misapprehension that the corruptions of the world—the hateful wrongs that have brought millions to such a pass of misery—are things in which Christendom has no part and that our own hands are clean. For the things that crucify Christ and wreck the whole world are the common sins of every day—self-centredness, pride, apathy, cynicism, slackness, unkindness, every temptation put in another's path, every wasted opportunity, every pitiful compromise of which we are ashamed—these are the nails and the spear-thrust and the cross. And will anyone deny, with Jesus hanging there, that sin is the critical enemy, the most dangerous insatiable thing in the world, and that he personally needs to be forgiven?

Our first question is answered. Is forgiveness necessary? It is the one thing needful.

III

THE IRREPARABLE PAST

The second question which determined the whole trend of apostolic preaching on this matter, and which still rises out of the depths of human need

[1] *Positive Preaching and the Modern Mind*, 38.

whenever men and women turn aside into the House of God from the dust and heat and bewilderment of life—the second question is, *Is forgiveness possible?*

Note how this question arises. A man argues: "Here is this world where rigid law holds sway. Effect follows cause automatically. As a man sows, so shall he reap. As he makes his bed, so he must lie in it. As he acts, so he must bear the consequences. The past is past, and out of his control. Where, then, can forgiveness come in? There is no hope nor chance of it. The thing is impossible."

This is the logical reading of the situation. For every evil deed cast into the stream of life is like a stone falling into a river: the ripples spread out in unchecked, widening circles to the furthest shore. Thus evil propagates itself inexorably. Before the sinner knows what has happened, it is away out of sight and beyond control. How can forgiveness break redeemingly into such a situation? There seems no opening for it at all.

That is the haunting fear, and life and literature are full of it. What the great masters of literature—from Aeschylus and Sophocles down to Shakespeare and Dostoevsky—are saying is this: "There is no road back to where you started from. That day, years ago, you made your choice: and to-day it is burning your hands, and you would like to throw it away, but you can't!" "Verily I say unto you," declared Jesus, "they have their reward." [1] For the tragic thing about sin is not that it fails of its goal, but precisely that it succeeds. The judgment is that

[1] Matt. vi. 2, 5.

a man has to choose, and that he chooses as he does, and that he gets what he has chosen, and ends up chained to it. "God," says Brunner, "accepts man's emancipation from Himself; He burdens him with it."[1] In the words of the Spanish proverb: "Take what you will, said God, take it—and pay for it." Or in the graver language of the Hebrew poet: "God gave them their request, but sent leanness into their soul!"[2] "Things and actions are what they are," declared Bishop Butler in a famous sentence, "and the consequences of them will be what they will be; why then should we desire to be deceived?"[3] "He that is unjust," says the Book of Revelation in words of terrible warning, "let him be unjust still: and he which is filthy, let him be filthy still."[4]

> The Moving Finger writes; and, having writ,
> Moves on: nor all thy Piety nor Wit
>   Shall lure it back to cancel half a Line,
> Nor all thy Tears wash out a Word of it.[5]

And so the idea has deeply rooted itself in many a mind that forgiveness is not possible.

IV

Restoring the Broken Relationship

Now it is essential at this point to get our definitions clear. We have to put away once for all the

---

[1] *Man in Revolt*, 134.
[2] Psalm cvi. 15.
[3] Butler, *Sermon upon the Character of Balaam*.
[4] Rev. xxii. 11.
[5] Fitzgerald, *Rubáiyát of Omar Khayyám*.

idea that forgiveness means "letting off." They misunderstand the Gospel completely who think this is
its chief concern. Put away the thought that being
pardoned means escaping all the consequences or
the penalty of sin: it rarely means that. The prodigal was forgiven; but that does not mean that
there were not months of slow and difficult readjust-
ment and rehabilitation. The crucial point, however,
is that the penalty will feel very different to a forgiven man and to one who has not accepted forgiveness; for the forgiven man will see in the things
he has to suffer a creative purpose, a positive way
of co-operating with God; and therefore the judgment itself will seem transformed. It will be seen
as mercy and not wrath. If the prodigal had to face
the consequences, at least he was at home. There
might be bitter things to be endured, but what
really mattered was that the broken relationship had
been restored. Now this is forgiveness. It is not
the remission of a penalty: it is the restoration of a
relationship. And the question is—is that possible?
Can the lost relationship be renewed? Or must the
sinner accept the fact that things can never now be
the same, "never glad confident morning again"?
Can he get back? Can he ever hope to say with
Bengel, "O God, there is nothing between us"?

Those who deny this are leaving out two
supremely important facts which the apostolic
preaching always put right in the centre.

On the one hand, *the actual testimony of the forgiven*.
"Argue against it as you like," so runs the apostolic
logic, "we know this thing is true—for God has

been forfeited. He proves Himself as Lord, who stands above the Law which He Himself has laid down. Hence the revelation of God as Lord is not fully completed in the prophetic revelation; it is only fulfilled where God, as the generous Giver, in His own Person intervenes in the distorted relation of man with Him, where He, who has royal claims, in royal sovereignty takes the part of the accused, and sets him free from the guilt which separates him, the sinner, from the Creator." [1] Therefore when Huxley bluntly announces, "There is no such thing as forgiveness"; when Bernard Shaw declares, "Forgiveness is a beggar's refuge, we must pay our debts"; when H. G. Wells says that the ultimate power is "a harsh implacable hostility," we can reply, "Thanks for the information, but it is not your hidebound logic, it is heaven's grace that reigns!" "Blessed be His grace," cried John Bunyan when this discovery broke upon him, "that Scripture would call, as running after me, 'I have blotted out as a thick cloud thy transgressions, and as a cloud thy sins.' Indeed, this would make me make a little stop, and, as it were, look over my shoulder behind me, to see if I could discern that the God of Grace did follow me with a pardon in His hand." [2] A vivid picture indeed—God thrusting His forgiveness on a soul that would scarce believe it possible!

Faust, in the old story, gambled with his soul: and an artist has painted a picture—a game of chess, Faust at one side, Satan at the other. The game in

---

[1] Brunner, *The Christian Doctrine of God*, Dogmatics, I. 148.
[2] *Grace Abounding*.

the picture is almost over, and Faust has only a few pieces left, a king, a knight, one or two pawns; and on his face there is a look of blank despair, while at the other side of the board the devil leers in anticipation of his coming triumph. Many a chess-player has looked at the picture and agreed that the position is hopeless; it is checkmate. But one day in the picture-gallery a great master of the game stood gazing at the picture. He was fascinated by the look of terrible despair on the face of Faust. Then his gaze went to the pieces on the board. He stared at them absorbed. Other visitors in the gallery came and went, and still he studied the board, lost in contemplation. And then suddenly the gallery was startled by a ringing shout: "It is a lie! The king and the knight have another move!" This we know to be true of the human struggle; this is implicit in our proclamation of God as the Father of Jesus Christ. No matter how hopeless apparently the position, *the King and the knight have another move.*

Thus when Kierkegaard pictures Barabbas becoming a Christian, will anyone say it is fantastic and unreasonable? [1] Even Judas—if at the eleventh hour he had gone to Calvary, if he had waited to see the Resurrection, if he had encountered the risen Christ—might have heard the word that came redeemingly to Peter: "Lovest thou Me?" [2] This is the word which obliterates and masters and makes free. And by Christ's authority, this is the word we preach.

[1] *Journals*, 69.   [2] John xxi. 15.

V

The Ethics of Pardon

We have looked, then, at these two questions which the apostolic preaching of forgiveness had to face. We pass now, finally, to a third question which was thrust upon the Church from the beginning. This, no less than the others, is crucial for our modern evangelism. *Is forgiveness right?* Is it ethical? Is it morally respectable?

Observe how this arises. If God passes over sin —so runs the argument—if He restores the relationship as though it had never been broken, if He pardons freely and unconditionally as the Gospel says, is He not encouraging sin? Is there not a danger that instead of saving the sinner He will be demoralizing him—that the standard will be lowered, not heightened? Is this not the highroad to the antinomian heresy? Is it not verging towards the debased evangelicalism of piety without ethics? In fact, is this not precisely the tendency that has brought down upon religion the fierce criticism of the Marxist who denounces it as an opiate, and the polite disdain of the world that insists above all else on being unsentimental and realistic?

Moreover, there is a deeper doubt about the Christian position, a more searching question-mark erected against the preaching of free forgiveness. If the consequences of our sins are carried by someone else, if Christ has to stand in our place and bear

the guilty load we should have borne—is that fair?
Is it fitting and just and moral?

> For lo! between our sins and their reward
> We set the passion of Thy Son our Lord.[1]

Is that right?

It is a real difficulty; and it is worth observing
that it is as old as the history of the Church. Read
the Epistle to the Romans, and see what happened:
good people came to the apostle Paul and warned
him—"This Gospel of absolutely free forgiveness
may be what you call 'evangelical'; but certainly it
is dangerous. For this is what sinners will say: 'If
God is all grace and mercy, why worry about sin?
Let us go on sinning, and grace will abound—God
will have all the more opportunities for being
gracious!'" So good people spoke to Paul. "Don't
risk preaching a Gospel like that," they said, "it is
hazardous! It is verging on being immoral." And
this difficulty has obtruded itself all down the
Christian centuries, and to many good people it is
acutely present still. So some have looked askance
at the Christian preacher, and have rejected the
Christian message. "It is not moral," they have
complained, "it can't be right!"

VI

The Alchemy of Grace

What is the answer? I would suggest three
answers to the challenge. One is this. If forgiveness meant that God were making light of sin—God

---

[1] William Bright.

meeting our guilty distress like a man who says to his neighbour, "Oh, never mind, it is of no consequence"—then it would be immoral, downright subversive of all moral values. *But never and nowhere does it mean that.* On the contrary, it is precisely in forgiveness that God's inflexible righteousness appears. It is at the very place where the divine pardon is bestowed that the divine wrath is endorsed. God shows the hatefulness of sin in the very act of cleansing it away. At the heart of the Christian doctrine of atonement stands the fact that if our sin has serious consequences for ourselves, it has terrible consequences for God. As Denney put it, "To take the condemnation out of the Cross is to take the nerve out of the Gospel." [1] We can see now why Jesus reacted so strongly, even violently, against Peter's attempt at Caesarea Philippi to deflect Him from His vocation of suffering. For to have offered the world redemption by an easier road than Calvary would have been to obscure the inevitable judgment of holiness upon evil, to compromise the very nature of God, and ultimately to leave men to the mercy of a universe of caprice and chaos. We shall have to look at this more closely in our next chapter, when we are thinking specifically of the preaching of the Cross. But in the meantime, I would simply express it like this. Was it making light of sin when Jesus said to a poor penitent woman kneeling at His feet, "I do not condemn thee for what has happened, I forgive thee, but—go and sin no more"? [2] Is it

[1] *The Second Epistle to the Corinthians* (Expositor's Bible), 222.
[2] John viii. 11.

making light of sin if, in the very moment of loving
the sinner, Christ's eyes—towards the sin that has
tried to wreck him—are "like a flame of fire"?[1] Or
let us put it like this. Is it making light of sin if a
father's hair has been turned grey by a son's sin
before the lad comes back? Is it making light of
sin if a mother, before welcoming the wanderer
home, has felt the sword of a terrible shame stabbing
and piercing her heart? These are but dim, remote
analogies. The question is: is it making light of sin
if Christ, being God incarnate, opposed it with His
life and condemned it by His death? Is it making
light of it, if all the fearsome consequences of the
judgment upon sin, which is what the New Testament means by "the wrath of God," are not and
cannot be simply annulled, as though mercy cancelled out justice, but rather have to be taken over
and borne by God Himself? Is it making light of it,
if every single act of forgiveness has—as Paul and
John and the writer of the Hebrews all proclaim—the
blood of the Lord upon it? It is the cost of forgiveness, a cost so prodigious and unthinkable, which re-
futes for ever the charge that forgiveness is immoral.

The second answer is this. Theoretically, a free
pardon might seem to be a condoning of sin and a
demoralizing of the sinner: *actually it has precisely
the opposite effect.* It is the greatest force for
righteousness in all the world. To exclaim *O felix
culpa!* might indeed sound immoral: but not when
the passionate gratitude of the forgiven completes
the cry—*felix culpa quae tantum et talem meruit habere*

[1] Rev. i. 14.

redemptorem. None knew this better than the apostolic preachers themselves, for they had experienced it. Thus it was with Peter after the denial. "I have wrecked my life," the man felt miserably, "I'll never in this world lift up my head again. I don't know how it happened, this beastly thing, but it did—and it is the end of everything." Then a voice spoke— "Simon, son of Jonas, lovest thou Me? Then feed My lambs, feed My sheep." [1] So Jesus commissioned him anew, and put His work back into this man's hands in perfect trust. It was this divine act of unquestioning forgiveness and perfect trust which took the broken and unstable creature, frustrated the devices of the particular private devil that had tried to ruin him, and fashioned him gloriously into the flaming and resolute apostle of the Book of the Acts, who could defy Annas and Caiaphas and all their tribe. This is the regenerative force of a great forgiveness. And there is no other moral dynamic in all the world that can compare with it. "O Jesus my Lord, who have trusted and forgiven me —I vow, God helping me, I will never, never break my troth with You again!" And that is salvation.

Let me give you these most moving words of Kierkegaard, describing his own experience: "I am a poor wretch whom God took charge of, and for whom He had done so indescribably much more than I ever expected, oh, so indescribably much more that I only long for the peace of eternity in order to do nothing but thank Him. As a man, personally I am, in a more than general sense, a

[1] John xxi. 15.

sinner who has been far along the road to perdition
—a sinner who nevertheless believes that all his sins
are forgiven him for Christ's sake, even though he
must bear the result of punishment; a sinner who
longs for eternity in order to thank Him and His
love." [1]   There is the spontaneously creative power
of the experience of redemption, the sanctifying force
of the divine justifying initiative.   In a passion of
adoring gratitude the pardoned man is now united
to the Christ who endured the Cross and despised
the shame to identify Himself with him.   "But I do
love thee," cried poor, foolish, blundering Othello
to his Desdemona, and in a far deeper sense it is the
forgiven sinner's cry to Christ—"But I do love
thee! and when I love Thee not, chaos is come
again!"

Is this too subjective? Then let me add a third
fact, a fact so thoroughly objective that it can finally
refute the suspicion of immorality attaching to the
Christian doctrine of forgiveness.   What God in
Christ did at the Cross was not only to elicit the
sinner's repentance and win his heart and remake
his will: *it was to redeem the whole sinful situation.*
It was to introduce into the tragic sequence of sin
and resultant blindness and hardening, leading on
to further sin and deeper darkness, a force capable
of shattering for the first time that vicious circle in
which the human race was bound and helpless.   The
Cross was the divine strategy which not only
arrested the malignant agelong drift of the despotism
of iniquity, but actually took the supreme achieve-

1 *Journals*, 257.

ment of the devil and made that the supreme vehicle of redeeming grace. And the method of this strategy was forgiveness. This is the only alchemy that turns evil to good, the wrath of man to the praise of God. And when we think remorsefully of the vast and tragic total of the consequences of sin which have entered into the stream of history and passed beyond human recall, let us remember that even these are not beyond the redeeming control of the power which once turned the hour of the darkness of hell into the dawn of the light of heaven, and a Cross into a throne.

VII

Of Such Is the Kingdom

Therefore I would urge those who have been called to the ministry of the Word: at all costs make this vital *kerygma* of forgiveness plain and clear, that all may understand. Yet, indeed, in the last resort it does not depend for its efficacy upon being understood. No one on earth can fully understand it, nor grasp its ultimate implications.

> None of the ransomed ever knew
>   How deep were the waters crossed,
> Nor how dark was the night that the Lord
>   passed through.[1]

It does not depend on being understood: it depends on being received *sola fide*, appropriated by the trustful childlike heart to which alone the Kingdom belongs.

[1] Elizabeth C. Clephane.

There is a very moving story told by Dr. Warr in *Echoes of Flanders* about a soldier who as a boy had run away from home, and had gone from bad to worse and fathomed most kinds of sin, until in his regiment he was deemed to be utterly incorrigible. But when one of the officers, as a last daring experiment, made the reprobate his servant, an almost magic transformation began; and in the end he threw his life away most gallantly for the man whose trust had changed him. As the darkness came down after the enemy attack, and his life was ebbing out, there came to him by some strange whim of memory the words of a prayer he had learned years before at his mother's knee and had quite forgotten through the reckless years of sin. Now, gasping for breath, he began repeating them; the stretcher-bearer heard the words, as of a tired child at the close of day:

> The day is done, O God the Son,
> Look down upon—Thy little one.
> O Light of light, keep—me this—night
> And shed—around—Thy presence bright . . .

And on the scarred face of the man whom no one loved there was a light like the radiance of heaven; and the words were trailing off into the silence, but the last words came—

> I need not fear—if Thou—art near,
> Thou art my Saviour—kind and dear . . .
> So happily and—peacefully—
> I lay me—down—to rest—in Thee . . .

So he crossed the river. And I doubt not Jesus was there to welcome him on the other side.

It does not depend for its efficacy on being understood, this Gospel of forgiveness. It depends on the faith that takes it like a child—for of such is the Kingdom of heaven. "Courage, my son," said Jesus —and they were among the most characteristic words He ever spoke, repeated once and again to souls in need—"Courage, your sins are forgiven!" [1] By all means in his power, the preacher of the Word must help men to understand that forgiveness, freely offered in the Gospel; but above all, he must help them to take it, as in the grace of God he has taken it himself.

[1] Matt. ix. 2 (Moffatt).

CHAPTER THREE

PROCLAIMING THE CROSS

> Quaerens me sedisti lassus,
> Redemisti crucem passus,
> Tantus labor non sit cassus.
> *Dies Irae.*

IT was Gerald Heard who said: "Newton banished God from nature, Darwin banished Him from life, and now Freud has banished Him from His last stronghold, the soul." I wish to introduce the theme of Preaching the Cross by suggesting that, if for great numbers of our contemporaries the effect of Newton, Darwin and Freud has been to banish the divine, it has even more emphatically been to banish the demonic. St. Paul's "principalities and powers"—the "spirit forces of evil" whose malignant grip upon the souls of men called forth "a second Adam to the fight and to the rescue"—are now known, we are told, to have been mere apocalyptic imagination.[1]

To this result Newton, Darwin and Freud certainly contributed. For Newton's work left no room for an irrational principle in nature; and the devil is essentially irrational, teleologically indefinable—as St. John marks by his significant use

---

[1] A few paragraphs from an article I contributed to the *Scottish Journal of Theology*, Vol. IV. No. 3, are included here by permission of the editors of the *Journal*.

of ἀνομία [1] and St. Paul by the phrase "the mystery
of iniquity." [2] "Only he who understands that sin
is inexplicable knows what it is." [3] Again, Darwin's
picture of the biological struggle for existence was
hailed as radically superseding the Biblical picture
of the cosmic struggle between the demons and the
kingdom of the Lord. Finally, Freud banished the
powers of darkness from their last stronghold, the
soul, by successfully dissolving them into psychological complexes, neuroses, and the like: so that
the good fight of faith becomes simply a matter of
inner individual adjustment.

I

GOD AND THE DEMONS

This elimination of the dimension of the demonic
has had its effect upon Christian theology. Take,
for example, the doctrine of man. In Romans vii
Paul interprets the human predicament with the
words "It is not I who do the deed, but sin that
dwells in me"— a usurping force, personal, alive,
tyrannical. On this James Denney cogently com-
ments: "That might be antinomian, or manichean,
as well as evangelical. A true saint may say it in
a moment of passion, but a sinner had better not
make it a principle." [4] This warning is entirely
salutary. But the fact remains that when a saint,
or for that matter a common sinner, says this thing

---

[1] I. John iii. 4.   [2] II. Thess. ii. 7.   [3] Brunner, *Man in Revolt*, 132.
[4] *Expositor's Greek Testament*, Romans, 641.

in a moment of passion, "It is not I who do the deed, but sin that dwells in me"—as though some outside force getting hold of him were ultimately responsible—it is at once much more Biblical and much nearer to the mark objectively than any psychological reinterpretation which suggests that Romans vii and the perpetual predicament there mirrored can be dealt with under some such formula as "the divided self." If temptation were essentially this kind of inner conflict—a higher self against a lower self—then presumably the temptations of Jesus in the desert and Gethsemane were also of this kind: which would make havoc of the Gospel.

I submit that in our Christian anthropology we have lost something vital here. Too much there has been lost the sense of a cosmic battle which emerges visibly on to the stage of world events— where it is not simply to be identified with what Herbert Butterfield has called "the gravitational pull in history," [1] and where it traverses and cuts clean across all such external and contingent frontiers as democracy and Communism and invades at deeper levels the arena of the life of man and the experience of the individual soul. We have lost the emphasis that what is really at issue in the agelong tragic dilemma of Romans vii, what in fact is always at stake in every moment of temptation, is not a higher self or a lower self, personal integrity or dishonour —that is the least of it: what is at stake is the strengthening or (please God) the weakening of the spirit forces of evil that are out to destroy the

[1] *Christianity and History*, 38.

kingdom of Christ. "For," says Calvin, "if the glory of God is dear to us, as it ought to be, we ought to struggle with all our might against him who aims at the extinction of that glory. If we are animated with proper zeal to maintain the kingdom of Christ, we must wage irreconcilable war with him who conspires its ruin." [1] This is the insight which modern theological reconstructions have been apt to lose. We have lost Paul fighting with wild beasts at Ephesus and Luther flinging his ink-pot at the devil.

It is, however, in respect of the doctrine of the atonement that this loss is most serious: and this is where the matter impinges upon our preaching of the Cross.

Those theologies which stress mainly or solely the revelatory aspect of the death of Christ—as though all that was needed by a sinful world was for God to show how much He loved it—have failed to take seriously the New Testament's concentration upon the demonic nature of the evil from which the world has to be redeemed. They have misunderstood as secondary and extraneous elements in the primitive Christian proclamation what in fact are integral and basic components of the Gospel.

It is, indeed, true that in the New Testament the Cross is set forth as the climax of revelation. And thus to set it forth must always be a primary concern of the preacher of the Gospel. It will be well, therefore, to fix our attention on this, before proceeding further.

[1] *Institutes*, I. xiv.

II

THE RENDING OF THE VEIL

Consider the synoptic statement, derived from the early predocumentary tradition, that in the moment when Jesus died "the veil of the temple was rent in twain from the top to the bottom." [1] This the evangelists took to mean the radical destruction of secrecy and exclusion. In this event was symbolized the laying bare of the very heart of God.

For the veil had been hanging there for years. It looked as if it might hang there for ever. Gorgeously embroidered in blue and purple and scarlet, the massive curtain hung before the inmost shrine; and it guarded its secret well. It was there to fulfil a double function. On the one hand, it was there to keep men out: a warning to sinful man that where the last mysteries of religion were concerned he must keep a respectful distance. On the other hand, it was there to shut God in; for behind that hanging veil there was silence deep as death and darkness black as night, even while the sun was blazing outside. It had been hanging there for years: it looked as if it might hang there for ever.

This was the heart of the Jewish cult. The Jew worshipping in the temple was sure there was something behind the veil. But what? That, none could clearly tell. Some divine presence, he imagined, was there in the dark, something numinous and awesome and formidable, the mystery of holiness, the terror

---

[1] Matt. xxvii. 51, Mark xv. 38, Luke xxiii. 45.

of the Lord. This was Judaism's *deus absconditus*. This was the perpetual frustration of man's search for the eternal. But one day Jesus died; and from top to bottom, declare the evangelists, the veil was rent. Here was the decisive revelatory event: man's agelong fumbling quest was at an end.

Now a great part of the urgency of preaching to-day lies in the fact that so many to whom we preach are back where those Jews were before this thing happened. They believe there is something behind the veil, some hidden power behind the world they see. But what? That is the haunting uncertainty. A living Mind, says one. An austere righteousness, says another. A heartless indifference, was Thomas Hardy's guess:

> The dreaming, dark, dumb Thing
> That turns the handle of this idle Show.[1]

In every congregation there are some who are wondering: Is He a God to whom it is worth my while to pray? Is He a God who knows the miseries of man and all the wrong and heartache of the world? Is He a God who can bring me hope and a new beginning when I have done something that makes me hate myself and leaves me feeling wretched and ashamed? These are the questions to which many a man is groping for an answer, and finding only an impenetrable veil. And the minister of the Gospel, seeking to help those who are burdened with these intolerable perplexities about life and providence and history and destiny, has to tell them there is no

[1] *The Dynasts.*

answer to their perplexities, none whatever, save in
the death of our Lord on Calvary.

This rends the veil, precisely because it is not
words nor theory nor idea, but a deed; an event—
as our argument has already emphasized [1]—at once
historic, unique, eschatological; God's mighty act
towering over the wrecks of time. It was not enough
that God should give the Promise, the Covenant, the
Torah; through the long centuries God had been
dealing thus with men, and the veil remained. It
was not enough that He should make His prophets
a herald voice to men; even the word of God burning
and flaming on their lips could not answer the
ultimate question; even "the hammer that breaketh
the rock in pieces" [2] could not drive home the final
truth. It was not enough to send Jesus preaching
the Sermon on the Mount, challenging and appealing
to men in tones they had never heard before to trust
God's love for everything; even that could not do
it. The veil of doubt still lingered. And then, when
it seemed that the last word had been spoken and
God could do no more, then Jesus died, and the veil
was rent in twain. The death of Christ gives me the
very heart of the eternal, because it is not words at
all, not even sublime prophetic utterance: it is an
act, God's act, against which I can batter all my
doubts to pieces. We preach Christ crucified, God's
truth revealed.

Notice, moreover, how this supplies the great
missionary motive of Christendom. Exclusiveness,
particularism, segregation—this was written into the

---

[1] See pages 17-28 above.   [2] Jer. xxiii. 29.

very structure of Temple religion. Inscribed before the eyes of every Gentile seeker after God stood the daunting words: "Whosoever passes this barrier will himself be the cause of the death which overtakes him." As for the Holy of holies behind the veil, only one man on one day in the year might enter there. Strange irony of fate that in Jesus' time that one privileged individual should have been a Caiaphas! And all the rest, even when heart and flesh were crying out for the living God, thwarted and thrust back by barrier after barrier, and finally by the unrelenting veil which it was sacrilege and death to touch! But the day of Calvary, declare the evangelists, destroyed the veil. It finished the monopoly. It broke through the alienation. Hence the missionary passion of apostolic preaching. Greek, barbarian, Scythian, bond, free, white, black—let them all come! "Think not to say"—in nationalist complacency—"we have Abraham for father; for God is able of these stones to raise up children unto Abraham." [1] The primitive Christian confession *Kyrios Christos*, as Cullmann has pointed out, implies universalism, "a radical totalitarian claim." [2] "Tell the King," cried Bishop Hannington of Uganda when the emissaries of the African chieftain came upon him to murder him, "tell the King that I open up the road to Uganda with my life!" We preach the Cross, for we have received Christ's commission: "Tell the world that I open up the road to God with My life!" This is everyman's highway. Let no man nor Church, no theology nor ecclesiastical decree,

[1] Matt. iii. 9.   [2] *Christ and Time*, 178.

seek to reimpose the restrictions and re-erect the
barriers which Jesus at so great a cost has levelled
to the dust.   For to close up a right-of-way is a
crime.

III

THE SINISTER COALITION

But now to proceed.   The apostolic *kerygma* never
stopped here, in this revelatory aspect of the death
of Christ.   It was concerned with something more
than the letting in of a light for men who sat in
darkness and the opening up of a road for aliens who
felt themselves excluded.   After all, what can a light
avail if men are blind and cannot see, or a road if
they are too lame to walk?   The really tragic force
of the dilemma of history and of the human predicament is not answered by any theology which
speaks of the Cross as a revelation of love and mercy
—and goes no further.   But the primitive and
Pauline proclamation went much further.   It spoke
of atonement, guilt-bearing, expiation.   It spoke of
all this as an objective transaction which had changed
the human situation and indeed the universe, the
kosmos itself.   In what Bishop Aulén has designated
the "classic" or "dramatic" theory of the atonement,[1] it spoke of the decisive irrevocable defeat of
the powers of darkness.   It spoke of the Cross—
"placarded" the Cross, as Paul put it to the Galatians [2]—as the place where three factors had met

---

[1] Gustaf Aulén, *Christus Victor*, 20 ff.   [2] Gal. iii. 1.

and interlocked: the design of man, the will of
Jesus, the predestination of God. Now all this is
crucial for contemporary evangelism. And here I
would raise the important question of emphasis, to
which reference has already been made. It seems to
me that the relevance of this threefold drama will be
fully understood only if we take quite seriously what
the New Testament has to say about the invisible
cosmic powers which seek to dominate history and
to control the wills and destinies of men. To this
too frequently neglected teaching of the New Testament we shall endeavour in what follows to give
due weight.

Behind the Cross there lay, first, *the design of men*,
a coalition of ascertainable historic forces. It was
the human attitudes of pride, self-love, traditionalism
and fear which, when worked out into social, political
and ecclesiastical magnitudes, resulted in the death
of the Son of God. Now it is vital to remark that
in the New Testament these visible historic forces
always appear as mere agents of other invisible
powers incalculably more sinister and dangerous.

It will be worth our while to analyse this situation
more closely.

Among those who numbered Jesus with the transgressors were the religious people of His day. This
was one element in the coalition which erected the
Cross. It is disconcerting but true that it was precisely those who were loudest in religious profession
who, on encountering Jesus, were loudest in censure
and protest. They saw Him healing on the Sabbath,
and they said He was undermining the law of Moses.

They heard Him speaking of destroying and re-
building the Temple, and they could not bear such
iconoclastic folly. They heard Him talk on the
deepest themes with measureless assurance and
authority: "What right has He to speak like this,"
they demanded, "this carpenter's apprentice out of
Nazareth? It's blasphemy!" They saw the dis-
reputable company He frequented, the notorious
creatures with whom He would spend hours in
conversation, the riff-raff and the under-dog to whom
He seemed particularly attracted; and they said with
stinging contempt, "This shows where His true
affinity is! Like draws to like—He has given Himself away: Friend of publicans and sinners!" When
organized religion thus branded Jesus as anarchic
and subversive, the Cross was coming in sight.

A second element in the coalition was politics,
both Jewish and Roman. On the Jewish side, it
looked at first as if Jesus might serve the nationalist
purpose by heading a movement of revolt, and then
no praise was too high for Him; but when that
hope turned out to be illusory, when it appeared that
He had misled the cause and betrayed the revolution,
disappointed vengefulness knew no bounds. What
right had this man to kindle the popular hopes, and
then—just when things seemed moving towards a
national uprising—leave them in the lurch? It was
a bitter business, to be thus hoodwinked and betrayed. On the Roman side, as represented by
Pilate, there could be only one reaction to the charge
of anti-Caesarism. Other accusations Rome could
afford to dismiss indulgently, but not this. Thus it

was that politics joined hands with religion to devise
the crucifixion.

The third element was the crowd. In any assess-
ment of responsibility for the death on the Cross,
the ordinary people—apathetic, easily manœuvred,
too lethargic to cast off the bonds of fate—must bear
part of the blame. Where were all the people who
had thronged round Jesus when His fame was
highest, the thousands who had once hung upon
His words? They had lost interest. Perhaps the
devastating candour of His moral challenge had been
too much for them. Never was the hateful power
of a resolute unscrupulous minority—in this case
Caiaphas, Annas and their confederates—to subvert
a tolerant, unorganized majority more evident than
on the night in which the crowd shouted for
Barabbas and sent Jesus to His death.

It is a commonplace to say that these same forces
—religious, political, social—are operating still to
crucify the Son of God afresh. Those people who
thus judged of Christ—religious people, power poli-
ticians, average citizens—were at bottom very like
ourselves; and when our religion grows complacent
(it often is), and our politics self-centred (they often
are), and our society apathetic to the great moral
and spiritual issues (it is often dreadfully apathetic),
then we are lining up exactly where those men stood
in relation to Christ, and the whole tragic situation
is recurring and being perpetuated. This we know.
This insight must always characterize our preaching
of the Cross. But what is not so frequently re-
marked is the New Testament's insight that behind

all these forces stand (in Pauline language) "the rulers of this world age, the potentates of the dark present." [1]

We have seen that organized religion was at the Cross. But the New Testament sees more deeply, and explains this by saying that in the "end time" which has now begun Antichrist appears, and that the really sinister thing about Antichrist is not (as might be supposed) his radical difference from Christ, but precisely his diabolical resemblance to Christ: he is so like Christ that he can successfully masquerade as Christ (as the word Anti-Christ itself suggests) and claim to stand in Christ's place, deceiving the very elect. Hence St. John's urgent warning about testing the spirits: Antichrist will not deceive those who possess the true "chrism." [2]

Politics were at the Cross. But again the New Testament sees more deeply, and declares that Herod and Pilate, the representatives of government, the duly constituted rulers of the day, were unwitting agents of powers greater than their own, greater even than the Roman State, namely, the invisible, spiritual, demonic "rulers of the present age": it was they, wrote Paul to the Corinthians, that "crucified the Lord of glory." [3]

And the average man was at the Cross. But once again the New Testament sees more deeply. For when the cry was raised, "His blood be on us and our children," what held these men in its baleful grip may have looked like necessity or expediency

[1] I. Cor. ii. 8, Eph. vi. 12.   [2] I. John ii. 18, 20.
[3] I. Cor. ii. 8.

or fate: but the New Testament rejects such
abstractions, and speaks rather of unseen spirits
besieging the very nature of man and perverting it
to serve their will. Necessity, expediency, defensible
strategy, the decree of fate—we heard all these
explanations in the days of Hiroshima and Nagasaki.
But when men and nations of decent average morality
are caught up and involved in such a situation,
driven by an almost irresistible compulsion in
directions in which they have no desire to go—
"another law in my members, warring against the
law of my mind" [1]—who can doubt that something
living and demonic is at work?

IV

Self-identification Unlimited

What then? Certainly this intensifies the serious-
ness of that warfare which is history. But does it
diminish hope? To answer this, we pass on now to
the second of the three factors which the apostolic
kerygma found interlocking in the Cross. If the first
was the design of men, the coalition of historic forces,
the second was *the will of Jesus Himself*. He chose
this open-eyed. It was His own deliberate act.
Could He save the suffering race of men and redeem
the enslaved only by getting right in amongst them?
Then right in amongst them He would go. It is
precisely this synthesis of suffering and royalty
which constitutes, as Rudolf Otto expresses it, the

[1] Rom. vii. 23.

"incomparable originality" of Christ.[1] He would identify Himself with men to the uttermost.

At every stage of the narrative this vehement resolve of self-identification can be seen at work.

Watch Him, for example, at John's baptism in the Jordan. Even the early Church (as Matthew's account makes clear) felt it strange that Jesus, the sinless One, should have submitted Himself to a baptism expressly designed for the remission of sins.[2] What had the Holy One of God to do with a confessional? Ought He not to have stood apart and said, "This is valid for sinners, but for Me irrelevant"? Then He would not have been our Saviour. What Jesus was doing that day at the Jordan was to identify Himself with the broken and the burdened, the unfortunate and the disinherited, making their troubles His trouble, their shame His shame, numbering Himself with the transgressors.

Or watch Him in the friendships He made—how He ranged Himself beside the Zacchaeuses, the Mary Magdalenes, not in any forced, official way, not in the tacit superiority of the morally religious who go about self-consciously doing good, but quite simply and directly, because He loved them so and was not ashamed to call them brethren.

Above all, watch Him as the story nears its end. Is it not symbolic that when He died at last it was between two thieves? All His life He had belonged to sinners; and in His death He was not divided from them. It is His chosen place.

In short, what is it we really see at Calvary? By

---

[1] *The Kingdom of God and the Son of Man*, 255.   [2] Matt. iii. 13 ff

whose will, whose action, was Jesus hanging there?
The will of Pilate, the design of Caiaphas, the act of
Caesar, the boasted triumph of the demonic dynam-
ism of principalities unseen—this is but a fragment
of the truth.   Did not Jesus speak that royal word—
"No man taketh My life from Me: I lay it down
of Myself"? [1] He could have avoided it. He was
repeatedly tempted to avoid it: tempted in the
desert; tempted by Peter—"This shall not be unto
Thee"—and how real that temptation was is manifest from the fierceness of the retort, "Get behind
Me, Satan"; [2] tempted in Gethsemane until His
sweat was great drops of blood. He did not need
to die. "Can I not pray to My Father, and He
shall give Me more than twelve legions of angels?" [3]
—the divine redeeming counterpart of the legions
of the demons. No helpless victim this! He could
have avoided it. But He chose not to avoid it. He
numbered Himself with the transgressors to bear
our sins away. It was in a willing passion of self-
identifying love that He gave Himself for me. "If
I make my bed in hell, Thou art there."

It is a strange thing surely that still at this time
of day there are people who call the doctrine of the
atonement immoral. "I don't want anyone suffering
for me and bearing my sins," wrote one of our
leading dramatists not so long ago: not seeing
apparently that such a statement was not merely
irreligious but actually unintelligent. For the fact
is that even on the purely human level it is just this
willing self-identifying of the strong with the weak,

[1] John x. 18.   [2] Mark viii. 33.   [3] Matt. xxvi. 53.

of the good with the bad, that is the world's hope. The principle can be seen at work in the patriot suffering for his country, in the research doctor sacrificing his own health for the victims of disease, in the philanthropist wearing himself out to ransom the downtrodden and oppressed, in the captain of a sinking vessel getting the women and children to safety and then going down with his ship. The man who protests "I want no one suffering for me" is ignoring the fact that not only religion but the whole of life is built that way. What Caiaphas said in cold, calculating cynicism—"It is expedient that one man should die for the people" [1]—may be the voice of the devil, as indeed it was on Caiaphas' unscrupulous lips. But looked at from another angle, it is the very truth of God. It *is* expedient—it always has been and always will be expedient—that one man should die for the people. David Livingstone, dying on his knees in darkest Africa; the X-ray pioneer losing limb or life for the advancement of knowledge and the relief of suffering; the Headmaster of an English school who during an air-raid marshalled his pupils into the shelters and then, going back to make sure that none had been left behind, was himself caught by a bomb and instantly killed—"one man dying for the people." This is the cosmic principle of love, the cruciform pattern on which life itself is built, the ground-plan of the universe.

Now in the teaching of Jesus Himself we have the warrant for expecting to find this same principle, which is inscribed all over the earth, written also

[1] John xi. 50.

over heaven. Here is a clue to the divine nature and
the divine action in history. "If ye do this," said
Jesus in one of His most frequent arguments, "If ye
—how much more God!" [1] If human love will thus
agonize to bless, how much more love divine!   I
think we should not be afraid to use this argument,
as though it might be a fallacy. It is at any rate the
logic of Christ. "If you would know," cried
Lacordaire, "how the Almighty feels towards us,
listen to the beating of your own heart, and add to
it infinity!" [2] "I want no one suffering for me and
bearing my sins," says the natural man. But he
cannot contract out of it. He is involved. How
much more God!

This, then, was the second factor at the Cross—
the will of Jesus. But here again there is a significant
New Testament emphasis which is too often overlooked. The New Testament insists that this will of
Jesus in His death is only to be understood in
relation to the invisible powers dominating the
universe and the life of man. The degree of humilia-
tion and sacrifice accepted in the Incarnation is not
to be measured simply by the fact that there the
Word was made flesh and became identified with
sinful humanity (as Hebrews puts it, "He who
sanctifieth and they who are sanctified must be all
of one group," [3]); beyond that stands the fact that
by His entrance into the world Jesus was brought
into contact with, and in some measure made subject
to, the invisible rulers of that world, and to one of

[1] Matt. vii. 11.   [2] Dora Greenwell, *Lacordaire*, 219.
[3] Heb. ii. 11, ἐξ ἑνὸς πάντες.

these in particular, namely, "him that had the power of death." [1] Christ's coming to earth, says Dibelius, was an advance into enemy-occupied territory. [2] It was only by meeting these forces on their own ground, only, that is, by getting into history where they were entrenched, that He could break their power.

This is indeed essential to the understanding of the drama unfolded in the Gospels. In St. Luke, the whole narrative of the activity of Jesus is enclosed, as Dibelius points out, by two onslaughts of Satan: at the outset in the desert, and at the last when "Satan entered into Judas." [3] It is clear that the Synoptic picture of the Temptation conflict, in which Jesus "bound the strong man" before "raiding his house," [4] is intended to set the key for everything that follows. Hence the sign that the Kingdom has come near is precisely the casting out of demons. [5] Hence Jesus' own interpretation of the results of the first mission preaching: "I beheld Satan as lightning fall from heaven." [6] Hence Jesus' chosen self-designation "Son of Man": for as it is in the soul of man, in Adam (to use the name generically), that the cosmic principalities and powers most clearly reveal their hand and exercise their demonic sway, so it must be by a second Adam, Son of Man, that that sway is finally broken. Hence, moreover, the word of the Johannine Christ, en-

---

[1] Heb. ii. 14. On this, cf. J. Weiss, *Der erste Korintherbrief,* 57.

[2] *Die Geisterwelt im Glauben des Paulus,* 202 : "ein Vordringen ins feindliche Lager."

[3] *Op. cit.* 203. Cf. Allan D. Galloway, *The Cosmic Christ,* 37 ff.

[4] Mark iii. 27.   [5] Luke xi. 20.   [6] Luke x. 18.

tering upon His Passion—"Now is the judgment of
this world: now shall the prince of this world be
cast out." [1] Hence the appalling, unthinkable
wrestling in Gethsemane. Hence the saying at the
arrest, "This is your hour, and the power of darkness." [2] When Jesus became obedient unto death,
even the death of the Cross, He did it in the con-
fidence that in this final act the dark powers would
overreach themselves and so be finished for ever:
had they known that, Paul suggests, they would
never have done it.[3] But this was the will of Jesus
in His death. In the words of P. T. Forsyth:
"The holiness of Christ was the one thing damna-
tory to the Satanic power. And it was His death
which consummated that holiness. It was His
death, therefore, that was Satan's fatal doom." [4]
Hence Paul was entirely right when with magnificent
daring he pictured Christ as the one who wielded
the hammer at Calvary: the bond was cancelled, he
told the Colossians, nailed to the tree. "He dis-
armed the principalities and powers, and made a
show of them openly, triumphing over them at the
Cross." [5] As Calvin puts it, commenting on these
words from Colossians, "There is no tribunal so
magnificent, no throne so stately, no show of
triumph so distinguished, no chariot so elevated, as
is the gibbet on which Christ has subdued death
and the devil, and trodden them under His feet."
He masters the whirlwind, and rides upon the storm.

It is here that the Pauline atonement theology

---

[1] ὁ ἄρχων τοῦ κόσμου τούτου.   [2] ἐξουσία τοῦ σκότους.
[3] I. Cor. ii. 8.   [4] *The Glorious Gospel*, 6.   [5] Col. ii. 15.

requires to be correlated with the basic doctrine of
union with Christ. As Jesus thus identifies Himself
utterly with the human race in its plight and bewilderment and confusion—put it more personally,
as Jesus identifies Himself with my trouble and
weakness and defeat, must I not now identify myself
with His sacrifice, His power, His victory? In such
an act, the transfusion of life becomes possible. He
takes my failure, my shame, my misery: I take His
strength, His purity, His peace. This is the true
"substitution," and it means the darkness routed
and the night gone and the glory of God risen
upon us. In Luther's words, *Tu, Domine Jesu,
es justitia mea, ego autem sum peccatum tuum.* [1]
"In faith," writes Brunner, "man ventures to be
most daring, to identify himself with Christ, because
Christ identifies Himself with him." [2] Then all
things are made new. This is in fact the faith that
justifies. For God judges men, not by legal
righteousness, but by their response to His righteousness in Christ; not, that is, by position, but by
direction; not by the fact that some are ethically
better equipped than others, but by the fact that
some have their faces to Christ and some their backs.

Herein, too, lies the redemption of history. "The
world's awful need," to quote P. T. Forsyth again,
"is less than Christ's awful victory. And the devils
we meet were all fore-damned in the Satan He
ruined. The wickedness of the world is, after all,
'a bull in a net,' a chained beast kicking himself to

---

[1] Quoted by Heim, *The Church of Christ and the Problems of the Day*, 92.
[2] *Man in Revolt*, 487.

death." [1] In these words written fifty years ago
Forsyth anticipated Cullmann, who in place of the
metaphor of the bull in the net speaks of the
"principalities and powers" between the Resurrection and the Parousia as tied to a rope, still free
enough to evince their demonic character, but nevertheless bound, since Christ has already conquered
all demons: the Cross and the Resurrection being
the decisive battle that has turned the tide of the
war and settled the issue, even though Victory Day
may still lie in a future out of sight.[2] May we not
say that the crucial illustration here is death itself,
"the last enemy"? Men still have to die; yet in the
Cross and Resurrection of Jesus death—this most
omnipotent of the principalities and powers—has
been finally conquered; so that of those who are
united with Christ and His victory it is true to say
that they "have passed out of death into life." [3]

V

The Paradox of the Purpose of God

We turn, finally, to the third factor in the death
of Christ which the apostolic *kerygma* never omitted.
If it saw at the Cross the interlocking of the will of
Jesus and the coalition of historic forces, it saw also
—and this was its deepest insight—*the predestination
of God*. And no evangelism will be valid, no preaching of atonement strong and effective, in which this
does not hold a central place.

It is conceivable that when the Cross first hap-

[1] *Op. cit.* 7.   [2] *Christ and Time*, 198.   [3] I. John iii. 14.

pened the immediate reaction might have been to
cry, "Why was God not there to prevent it? Had
God been there this tragedy need never have happened." But what the first Christians came to
see was this—that God was there as nowhere else.
This thing occurred, declared Peter in the first
Christian sermon, just after Pentecost, "by the
determinate counsel and foreknowledge of God."[1]
They never preached the Cross without saying,
"This is God's deed, God's purpose in action, God's
way of bringing a mad and ruined world back to
health and sanity and peace." As John Calvin put
it, "Had it not been by God's will that Christ was
crucified, where were our salvation?"

This is the Gospel whose divine dramatic paradox
is too startling for the wisdom of men. In Paul's
own day they called it "scandal," "foolishness":
"unto the Jews a stumbling-block, and unto the
Greeks sheer absurdity";[2] and the offence persists.
Men have stood at the Cross and impeached the
Governor of a universe in which such a desperate,
unpardonable deed could be perpetrated. "Don't
you know," cries one of Dostoevsky's characters,
looking at a painting of the Crucifixion, "a man
might lose his faith by looking at that picture?"
"That is what is happening to me," is the reply.
And indeed from the angle of what Paul calls "the
wisdom of the world," the Cross is simply the
focusing-point of the whole terrible enigma of the
callousness of providence and the malevolence of
fate and all the cruel injustice of the world. If there

[1] Acts ii. 23.   [2] I. Cor. i. 23.

are many things, broods the Persian poet darkly, for which we poor creatures need to be forgiven by God, there are some at least for which God needs to be forgiven by us! [1]

The question is—why did the disciples not feel thus about the Cross? If the Jew looked at the Cross and said, "It is a scandal! I require a sign, a work of power, and you offer me this pathetic symbol of defeat. Take it away"; if the Greek looked at it and said, "Folly and absurdity! I want wisdom, a rational explanation of life, and in the name of all that is irrational you offer me this ridiculous anomaly. Take it away"—why did not the apostles feel like that?

Because, through the Holy Spirit given at Pentecost, they had seen past the moralism of the Jew and the intellectualism of the Greek to the eternal purpose of God. With awe and amazement they had grasped the overwhelming truth that this sacrifice of the Cross was no mere propitiation offered from earth to heaven: for the Sufferer was the second Person in the Trinity, God manifest in the flesh. If ever God had acted in history, He had acted then. In other words, the only valid doctrine of atonement is that which is linked to a full New Testament Christology. "In Christ," said Paul sublimely, "God was reconciling the world." [2]

What is the significance of this for the Biblical emphasis on the "principalities and powers"—that

---

[1] For all the Sin wherewith the Face of Man
Is blacken'd, Man's Forgiveness give—*and take!*
Rubaiyát.

[2] II. Cor. v. 19.

neglected aspect of New Testament thought which
we have stressed throughout this chapter? The
significance is that dualism is eliminated. To speak,
as the New Testament does, of an invisible empire
of evil over against the kingdom of Christ might
seem to indicate a dualistic interpretation of the
universe. But at point after point the New Testament safeguards itself against that position.[1] Thus
the pre-existence of Christ means that He was before
the angelic rulers, before creation itself: "in Him
all things were created," writes Paul to the Colossians, and specifically mentions the principalities and
powers which, casting off their original allegiance,
revolted into demonism.[2] Having been created "in
Him" they are essentially subject powers. Dualism
is further excluded by the insight of the New
Testament that in the death of Jesus the divine
sovereignty is such that the hostility of these powers
is compelled to subserve God's ends and not theirs.[3]
Their fierce antagonism becomes precisely the
vehicle for world redemption; and in the resurrection and exaltation Christ's victory is so far-
reaching and complete that He can actually use
these now subject forces and send them out as
emissaries to do His bidding: "Are they not all
ministering spirits?" asks the writer to the Hebrews.[4]

---

[1] Even the Jewish Rabbis did the same: the angels, they pointed out,
were created on the second or later days, not on the first, and therefore
had themselves no part in creation (Dibelius, *op. cit.* 189).

[2] Col. i. 16.   [3] I. Cor. ii. 8.

[4] Heb. i. 14. It is significant that Dibelius in *Die Geisterwelt im
Glauben des Paulus* interprets in this way even the ἐξουσίαι of Romans
xiii, seeing behind the government authorities the higher angelic
powers.

In the great passage in Philippians ii, where Paul is possibly quoting an early Christian hymn, the Lordship of Christ is displayed precisely by the fact that among those who bow the knee to Him are "beings celestial, terrestrial, and subterranean."[1] This is the negation of dualism. In the end, the same invisible powers are the tribute which the Son hands over to the Father, "that God may be all in all."[2]

Thus the preaching of the Cross requires a full New Testament Christology. The redeeming sacrifice is wrought out not only on earth but in heaven. It does not begin with Gethsemane and Pilate's judgment hall, nor even with Bethlehem and the squalor of the stable: it begins at the throne of God. The Suffering Servant who deals with evil by taking its full effect upon Himself is the express image of the person of God.[3] That is to say, the inexorable terrible consequences of the divine judgment upon sin are not abrogated, but borne by God Himself. Here at least the traditional translation of Revelation xiii. 8 (though doubtful exegetically) represents a cardinal truth: "The Lamb is slain from the foundation of the world." And if there are those to-day who would dismiss the apostolic Christology as a remote, unpractical irrelevance, we have to reply that it is the one faith big enough to make an impact either on the Roman Empire in the first century or on the miseries of the world in the twentieth. No doubt it is difficult to formulate. Men have stumbled and stammered before the glory of it for nineteen hundred years. But how much

[1] Phil. ii. 10. [2] I. Cor. xv. 28. [3] Heb. i. 3, Col. i. 15.

better surely to hold this flaming, magnificent truth
—which is the central truth of the New Testament
—to hold it by a robust and daring faith, than to
potter about with timid, reduced, de-supernaturalized
versions of it, which have not dynamic enough to
save a single soul, much less be the propitiation for
the sins of the whole world!

Behind Calvary is the throne of heaven. And if
we have seen God acting at the Cross with power
and great glory, if to that conquering grace we have
yielded up our souls in absolute, irrevocable commitment, then every suffering is transmuted, every
despair is pierced through with hope; and bright
against the dark background of the menace of the
mystery of evil, we see the glory of the Kingdom
that is to be.

VI

Not Against Flesh and Blood

One other practical note to conclude this chapter.
Were Paul to come back to-day and look upon the
tragic conflict of our world, he would still say that
"our wrestling is not against flesh and blood,"[1] not
against any group of men or nations, Caesarism or
Communism, as though the interests of democracy
were synonymous with the righteousness of God;
it is nothing so simple and naïve as that—God pity
the facile imagination which assumes our own
policies are blameless and our own hands clean. No,
the real warfare cuts across all such alignments, and

[1] Eph. vi. 12.

lies deeper down in the invisible realm where sinister forces stand flaming and fanatic against the rule of Christ. And the only way to meet that demonic mystic passion is with the δύναμις and passion of the Lord. Was it not Christ's declared intention to kindle that flame in human hearts? "I am come to send fire on the earth." [1] For only Spirit can conquer spirit. The children of darkness are wiser in this than the children of light. The devil knows better than stifle emotion. And it is no use, in a day when spirit forces of passionate evil have been unleashed upon the earth and when fierce emotions are tearing the world apart, it is no use having a milk-and-water passionless theology: no good setting a tepid Christianity against a scorching paganism. The thrust of the demonic has to be met with the fire of the divine. As indeed it can: since Christ has overcome the world.

[1] Luke xii. 49.

Chapter Four

PROCLAIMING THE RESURRECTION

Most glorious Lord of Lyfe! that, on this day,
Didst make Thy triumph over death and sin;
And having harrow'd hell, didst bring away
Captivity thence captive, us to win:
This joyous day, deare Lord, with joy begin;
And grant that we, for whom thou didest dye,
Being with Thy deare blood clene washt from sin,
May live for ever in felicity!

EDMUND SPENSER.

WE saw in the first chapter of this study that when the earliest Christian missionaries went out from Jerusalem to face the world they did so with the startling declaration—"The hour cometh, *and now is*." The new age, long expected by seers and prophets, had broken in from the beyond. The *eschaton* had projected itself from the remote future into the immediate present. The time was fulfilled, and God was fashioning His new creation.

I

THE CORE OF THE GOSPEL

Now the driving power behind this revolutionary belief was the fact of the Resurrection. This was indeed the very core of the apostolic *kerygma*. To be an apostle meant to have been an eye-witness of the Resurrection. It was the theme of every Christian sermon; it was the master-motive of every act of Christian evangelism; and not one line of the New

Testament was written—this is a point which cannot be too strongly emphasized, especially in view of modern attempts to bring the New Testament within the orbit of a humanistic social idealism—not one sentence, whether of Gospels, Epistles, Acts or Apocalypse, was penned apart from the conviction that He of whom these things were being written had conquered death and was alive for ever. "It is the Jesus who proved Himself to be the Christ in the Resurrection, whose earthly life and words are to be narrated." [1]

Never did the apostles make the mistake, all too common to-day, of regarding the Resurrection as a mere epilogue to the Gospel, an addendum to the scheme of salvation, a providential afterthought of God, a codicil to the divine last will and testament. This is to falsify disastrously the whole emphasis of the Bible. Not as an appendix to the faith was the Resurrection ever preached in the apostolic Church. The one and only God the apostles worshipped was the God of the Resurrection. The one and only Gospel they were commissioned to preach was the overpowering, magnificent good news of the Resurrection. In Denney's words, "It is the first and last and dominating element in the Christian consciousness of the New Testament." [2] Without the Resurrection, the Passion itself would be robbed of meaning. Without this, the whole Christian structure falls to pieces, and all talk of atonement is

[1] Brunner, *The Christian Doctrine of God*, Dogmatics, I. 37. Cf. *The Mediator*, 574: "The Gospels depict Jesus as only they could depict Him who had really experienced Him as the Risen Lord."
[2] *Studies in Theology*, 49.

empty words, "vanity of vanities." Paul was right: without this, our faith, our hope, our preaching are all vain.[1] Advent, Christmas, Epiphany, Good Friday are helpless to save.

Here it is worth emphasizing that it was no mere interest in immortality which explains this apostolic concentration on the Resurrection. It was not as a dramatic verification of personal survival that they preached Christ risen from the dead. They were not really concerned with proofs and theories of survival as such. All that was irrelevant. They preached the Resurrection as an eschatological, that is, as a cosmic event. When Christ left the grave, it was not merely an announcement that there is a hereafter and a life beyond—which in any case they knew already; it was the shattering of history by a creative act of God Almighty. In this cosmic event, as Paul saw and proclaimed, God was doing something comparable only with what He had done at the first creation. This was the beginning of a new era for the universe, the decisive turning-point for the human race. "The first Adam was made a living soul: the second Adam was made a life-giving Spirit." [2] The Resurrection meant that the world had died in the night and had been reborn. When Paul met the risen Christ on the Damascus road, the blinding thing about the encounter—it literally blinded him for three days—was that in that moment he looked face to face, without any veil between, upon the eternal purpose of God. Thus the apostles went out to preach, knowing that in the Resur-

---

[1] I. Cor. xv. 14.   [2] I. Cor. xv. 45.

rection the new age had arrived, and that this stupendous miracle signified the storming of history and the transforming of the world.

Not that they explained how it had happened. The modern man who demands such an explanation before he will believe does not know what he is asking. For if what death meant to Jesus as Son of God can never be measured in human reckoning, how should we be able to define the mode and manner of the Resurrection? That He who knew no sin should be subject to death which is sin's wages, that He who came forth from eternity should become obedient to that crisis which is the mark of finitude, that contradiction which conditions all historical existence—this defies every attempt to assess its significance for Christ. Here indeed it is literal truth to say that "none of the ransomed ever knew" the price paid by the Ransomer. How much more must the Resurrection baffle explanation! If we could explain the method by which on that day death was swallowed up in victory, it would simply mean that no real victory was won. The apostles were not concerned with explanations. Sometimes indeed they tried to follow Christ crucified, dead and buried, to go after Him in thought and imagination into that obscure world beyond the grave. "He descended into Sheol," they said. Doubtless they were remembering another picture from a bygone age, the prophet Isaiah's picture of another king, the king of Babylon the Great, who had gone down, when his day was over, into that dim region of the departed and had been taunted by its shadowy inhabitants: "Art thou become as weak as we? Art thou become like unto us? How hast thou fallen from heaven, O daystar, son of the morning!" [1] But now One had entered there against whom the gates of Sheol could not prevail. "It was not possible that He should be holden of death." [2] "As once Samson had come out from Gaza carrying the brazen gates upon his shoulders, so the 'most glorious Lord of life' came up out of hell, having broken down its gates." [3] He led captivity captive.

But precisely how it had happened the apostles did not seek to explore. It was the mighty act of God: but beyond that, they were content to leave the method of it veiled in mystery. Certainly their insight that Good Friday and Easter were not two events, but one indivisible mighty act of God, delivered them from the danger of a double standard of realism as though the Resurrection were somehow less factual than the Crucifixion. There is indeed a truth in Bultmann's insistence on the supra-historical character of the Resurrection: here is something which, though presented to us as a story within the framework of history, is actually above and beyond all historical categories. Here is eternity expressed in terms of time, the things on the other side in terms of this side. But when the argument goes on to maintain that the New Testament has to be "de-mythologized" before its Resurrection proclamation can be stated in existential terms, and that what we call the outer history of our redemption has

---

[1] Isaiah xiv. 10, 12.   [2] Acts ii. 24.
[3] Nathaniel Micklem, *What is the Faith?*, 177.

to be stripped off as an external shell before we can
reach the kernel of truth, then we have to retort
that this is making the Resurrection mean something
radically different from what those who first celebrated
it knew it to be: a bleak and depressing prospect
indeed for modern evangelism. The de-mythologiz-
ing school is perhaps not so modern as is generally
supposed. Certainly some of its manifestations bear
a curious resemblance to elements in ancient gnos-
ticism. And what some present-day theologies do not
understand is this—that the docetic tendency which
they themselves would disown as heresy when it
touches the Cross cannot suddenly become respectable as an interpretation of the Resurrection.

But now to proceed. If the apostles were content
to leave the method of the Resurrection veiled in
mystery, they knew themselves to be sons of the new
age it inaugurated. It was creatively and dynami-
cally related to the history of the race. The Resurrection was evidence that there had now appeared,
in the midst of time, life of a new dimension and
the baptism of eternity. The heralds of the Resurrection were not merely preaching it as a fact: they
were living in it as in a new country. They had
received a Kingdom which could not be shaken.
Through the open gates of Christ's empty tomb they
had come to their citizenship and entered into life.
In the words of the psalmist, they were men "born
in Zion." [1] "When Thou hadst overcome the
sharpness of death, Thou didst open the Kingdom
of Heaven to all believers."

[1] Psalm lxxxvii. 4, 6.

This is our Gospel. For this is what Christianity essentially is—a religion of Resurrection. This is what every worshipping congregation is intended in the purpose of God to be—a community of the Resurrection. This is the basic character of every act of public worship—a proclamation of the Resurrection. And this is what the Gospel offers to our dark and ruined chaos of a world, where men peering into the future are daunted by the well-nigh impossible task of creating order out of confusion and life out of death: the power of the Resurrection. "O rejoice that the Lord is arisen!"

It is true, of course, that for us Christians the Cross must ever stand at the very heart of things. If we bungling, sinful creatures lose sight of the Cross even for a day, we are done for—and we know it. But men may gaze at the Cross and miss the Gospel that saves, if they are still on the wrong side of Easter. It is a strange thing that volumes have sometimes been written on the theology of the Atonement which stop short at the Cross, ignoring the Resurrection or relegating it to a very secondary place. The effect of such works is unsatisfying and depressing. For there is no such thing as atonement and reconciliation apart from the Resurrection. "The Easter festival," writes Aulén, "has always been the central stronghold of the classic view of the Atonement." [1] This is the Christian symbol— not the dead Figure of the crucifix, but Christ risen, trampling a broken Cross beneath His feet. "Neither is there salvation in any other." [2]

---

[1] *Christus Victor*, 115.   [2] Acts iv. 12.

It might indeed be asked: What then becomes of Paul's deliberate assertion to the Corinthians, "I determined not to know anything among you, save Jesus Christ, and Him crucified"?[1] Such a declaration might appear to justify those treatments of the atoning work which focus all attention on the earthly ministry of Jesus and the Cross in which it culminated, and either omit the Resurrection altogether or else bring it in only as an epilogue not essential nor integral to the drama of redemption. But this would be seriously to misunderstand the apostle's meaning. For "knowing Christ" means here precisely what it means regularly in Paul: the primary reference is not to the Jesus of history but to the exalted, ever present Lord. Hence the historic phrase "knowing Christ and Him crucified" indicates the direction of the apostle's thought: it is moving, not—as is often supposed—forward through the earthly life to the final act on Calvary, but backward from the risen life to the sacrifice which lay behind it.[2] Christ alive for ever—this is the viewpoint at which Paul takes his stand to gaze upon the Cross; and to preach "Christ and Him crucified" is emphatically a Resurrection *kerygma*. We need to recapture this emphasis. It is one thing to preach the Cross as the last word of divine revelation. It is quite another thing to preach it as the road travelled once for all by One now known to be alive for ever. This was the stupendous reality behind

---

[1] I. Cor. ii. 2.

[2] This is brought out admirably by Professor John Knox, *Chapter in a Life of Paul,* 131.

the onward march of first century evangelism; and
nothing else in the twentieth century will rejuvenate
the Church and make its mission strong.

II

Modern Culture and Resurrection Faith

But now comes the question—How are we to
preach it? For our main concern in these pages is
with Biblical homiletics. How are we to present
the message to this generation? And what response
in the twentieth century is the apostolic *kerygma*
likely to elicit?

Let me take you back for a little to one famous
occasion when the Resurrection was preached in
Athens.[1] It is worth trying to visualize the scene.
For what happened that day was not simply an
itinerant evangelist addressing a wayside congregation. It was not just one more early Christian
sermon. It was something much more dramatic. It
was the encounter of two rival interpretations of life.
It was the clash and the collision of two great tidal
waves of history.

Here was Athens, sophisticated, questioning,
speculative Athens; and here was this little Jew
with his uncouth accent and his burning eyes. Here
was the heart of classical culture; and here was this
man of one explosive theme—God incarnate, crucified and risen. Here was the Hellenic philosophic
temperament, and here the Hebraic prophetic fire.

---

[1] Acts xvii. 16 ff.

Here was Mars Hill; and here, challenging it, the hill of Calvary. Here was the Mount of the Areopagus, and here the Mount of Zion. When Paul stood up that day in Athens to preach Jesus and the Resurrection, two worlds had met. The voice of prophecy was being fulfilled: "Thy sons, O Zion, against thy sons, O Greece." [1]

Yet certainly Acts xvii is unusual. This semi-philosophical discussion of human brotherhood, embellished with literary allusion and poetical quotation, is not the Paul we are accustomed to. Of course, what Luke has given us is only a summary of the apostle's Areopagus discourse; but as it stands, there is no mention of the Cross and the Resurrection until the very end. Paul does not pull out the diapason stop till the closing bars. The characteristic trumpet-note does not come till the final sentences. The first part of the sermon sounds more like a college lecture on the psychology of religion. It is as if Paul were saying to himself, "Do these Athenians like rhetoric, poetry, pantheism? They shall have it!" And so here, surprisingly, you have Paul the pantheist, Paul the purveyor of innocuous sentiments, Paul the quoter of Greek poetry.

But now, notice, there comes a point where you almost see him halting in his stride, as if saying, "Enough, Paul, of these copybook maxims, enough of these religious generalities!" And with that he puts the Resurrection trumpet to his lips. "Men of Athens, I am here to tell you that God has broken through into history. God has raised up Christ and

[1] Zech. ix. 13.

by this deed has changed the whole human situation and the universe itself radically and decisively. He has vindicated righteousness, and defeated the dark powers for ever!"

It was then that things really began to happen in Paul's congregation. And this is what is so significant for our modern evangelism.

Up to this point, they had stood listening, admiring, approving. As long as Paul stuck to pantheist generalities and humanist sentiments, they were on his side. "It is so much more comfortable," writes Brunner, "to have a pantheistic philosophy of life than to believe in a Lord God, because a pantheistic philosophy does not commit you to anything, but faith in the Lord God means obedience to His will. A God who is neuter makes no claims; He simply allows Himself to be looked at. A 'philosophy of life' instead of faith means aesthetic enjoyment instead of obedience." [1] It is perhaps therefore not surprising that the moment Paul shifted his ground, the moment he passed on from the harmless vagueness of natural theology to the pointed precision of the religion of Christ, the tolerant unanimity of his audience broke up into dissension. Every herald of the Resurrection to-day ought to ponder this. It is the situation Kierkegaard describes: "The moment I take Christianity as a doctrine and so indulge my cleverness or profundity or my eloquence or my imaginative powers in depicting it, people are very pleased; I am looked upon as a serious Christian. The moment I begin to express existentially what I

[1] *Man in Revolt*, 432.

say, and consequently to bring Christianity into
reality, it is just as though I had exploded existence
—the scandal is there at once." [1]

At Athens the reactions were varied. "When
they heard of the Resurrection, some mocked." It
was all so foreign, so clean outside the accustomed
orbit of their thinking, so wildly remote from their
rooted and settled preconceptions. "God does not
break into history," they jeered. "Righteousness
made regnant? Death abolished? What a fabri-
cated tale! Has the fellow no eyes to see, no sense
to realize that unrighteousness is still cynically ram-
pant, and that death still stalks through the world?"
Perhaps they became positively flippant. "That is
the worst of these Jews: they will persist in taking
life and death, themselves and God, so frightfully
seriously! It is so dull and tedious. This man Paul
now, it would do him good to go to school with some
of our Epicureans: they have got hold of the right
end of the stick, with their frank hedonistic zest and
gaiety and their amusing schemes to drive dull care
away." "When they heard of the Resurrection,
some mocked."

It is a familiar sound: the wisdom of this world
jeering at the wisdom of God, the pride of reason
denouncing the credibility of the faith as the credulity
of the faithful. Preach an abstract pantheism, and
no one will disturb you. Preach an impersonal
God—the sum-total of the ethical and religious
values—and you will be left in peace. But Resurrection—this is another matter. This is the

scandal. This is the palpable absurdity. These Christians—how credulous they are! Twenty centuries have echoed the laughter of the Areopagus. Here in the Resurrection of Jesus is the fact which at the first launched Christianity upon the world and conquered the throne of the Caesars; here is the rock on which the Church was built and has stood for two thousand years; here is the good news which, a million times, has dried the tears of the desolate and solaced the bruised heart's dumb agony; and —some mock.

> Loud mockers in the roaring street
>   Say Christ is crucified again:
> Twice pierced His gospel-bearing feet,
>   Twice broken His great heart in vain.
>
> I hear, and to myself I smile,
> For Christ talks with me all the while.[1]

And what can we do but "speak what we do know, and testify what we have seen," [2] and bear witness to what we have experienced? This at any rate was the way the apostles took in their preaching. The evidence they offered was neither signed statements of neutral observers nor closely reasoned philosophic argument: it was the evidence of lives changed utterly by contact with the risen Christ. And to-day if anything will shake and persuade the mocker, perhaps it will not be our arguments: it will be the degree of our own conviction. And that depends always upon the reality of our personal commitment to the risen Lord.

---

[1] Richard le Gallienne, *The Second Crucifixion.*
[2] John iii. 11.

But amongst Paul's listeners were others whose reaction was different. "When they heard of the Resurrection, some said, We will hear thee again of this matter." I used to think this was just polite evasion, the eternal refuge of the procrastinating spirit. I am not so sure of it now. I think they were really touched and moved by the dramatic *kerygma*. This Resurrection message—righteousness vindicated, captivity led captive, death and the demons defeated—they wanted to believe it. For that pagan world was in the grip of fear. Neither philosophy nor mythology, neither astrology nor mystery cult, had been able to roll back the dark shadow of irrevocable fate. The race was in bondage to a destiny decreed and fixed for ever in the unfriendly stars, and the terror of a hostile cosmos held the human spirit in thrall. So these men at Athens resolved to hear the apostle again; for wistfully they hoped his message might be true.

One of our great secret allies in the proclamation of the Word to-day is this same wistfulness, which neither a confident secularism nor a sterile fatalism can quite eradicate. "Religion," wrote Everard Meynell, "seems always to be setting its beneficent ambush for those who thought themselves most securely on another road." [1] In St. Augustine's words, *Ego fiebam miserior et tu propinquior*.[2] This unrest of the spirit Brunner describes as "difficulty of breathing—*angustiae*—the suffocating distress which the soul feels in its separation from God." [3]

---

[1] *The Life of Francis Thompson*, 250.   [2] *Confessions*, VI. 26.
[3] *Man in Revolt*, 195.

"All the miseries of man," wrote Pascal, "prove his grandeur; they are the miseries of a dethroned monarch." [1] How often one can detect in modern scepticism an undertone of the nostalgia of faith!

If someone said on Christmas Eve,
    "Come; see the oxen kneel,
In the lonely barton by yonder coomb
    Our childhood used to know,"
I should go with him in the gloom,
    Hoping it might be so. [2]

Moreover, to-day as in Paul's world there is a restlessness which can be traced back to fear. Man is afraid of the cosmos which his own science has disclosed, afraid of the forces his researches and technology have unleashed, afraid of his boasted freedom and of the destiny he has fashioned for himself, afraid because of his disobedience to the laws of God. "We will hear the Gospel again on this matter." That is what thousands in their hearts are saying. "We will reconsider Christ." And it is to such that Jesus says, as to His own wistful groping followers long ago, "Handle Me and see!" [3] "They looked unto Him," says an old Scripture, "and were lightened and their faces were not ashamed." [4]

Observe, finally, the third group on Mars Hill. "When they heard of the Resurrection, some mocked. Some said 'To-morrow.' Howbeit some clave unto him, and believed." They suddenly knew, listening to that heart-piercing Easter Gospel,

---

[1] *Pensées*, I. iii.   [2] Thomas Hardy, *The Oxen*.
[3] Luke xxiv. 39.   [4] Psalm xxxiv. 5.

"This is what all our life we have been seeking! At last the great secret is revealed." And gradually there dawned upon them the revolutionary consequences of their discovery. No more helpless submission to the triumphs of iniquity! No more corroding pessimism and disillusionment! No more "Vanity of vanities, all is vanity"! No more bondage to the savagery of death! All this was gone for ever; for now the Resurrection had put the key into their hands. Now the vain groping and fumbling in the dark were finished. Now they could arise and shine, knowing that their light was come, and that the glory of the Lord was risen upon them.

III

A Full Christology

This is our Gospel. In order to preach it in its fulness, we must give heed to certain fundamental notes in this Resurrection *kerygma* of the apostles.

One is *Christological*. In the preceding chapter I endeavoured to show that the Cross has redemptive significance only because of the Person of Him who died on it; only a real incarnation can provide a real atonement. So now, on the other side, I would underline the fact that always, when the apostles speak of the bridge constructed between God and man by the advent and sacrifice of Christ, the Resurrection is seen to be the keystone of the arch. This is the significance of the primitive Christian Confession which Paul cites at the beginning of Romans:

Christ, he asserts, was "designated Son of God with power by the Resurrection from the dead." [1] Brunner has expressed it memorably in his great picture of the parabola of redemption.[2] A parabola extends in two directions: the gradient comes steeply down from above, but "when it has reached the lowest point of the curve it strains upward again to return to the region whence it came." In the sacrifice of Christ, it is our desperate plight that determines the steepness of the gradient: the lowest point of the curve must pass through the fearful pit and the miry clay. "He emptied Himself," says Paul, "taking the form of a servant, being born in the likeness of men; and being found in human form, He humbled Himself and became obedient unto death, even death on a cross." [3] But before this movement can have redemptive force "this deepest point must also be the turning-point where the descent turns into the ascent." "The movement is from God *to God*." [4] "Therefore God has highly exalted Him and given Him the name which is above every name . . . that every tongue should confess that Jesus Christ is Lord, to the glory of God the Father." [5] "Therefore the message of Easter *is* the Christian message, and the Christian Church is the Church of the Resurrection." [6]

In these days when the humanist reduction of Christianity is so prevalent, it is vital that we should preach the Resurrection in its full Christological

---

[1] Rom. i. 4.   [2] *The Mediator*, 561.
[3] Phil. ii. 7, 8. Paul may here be quoting an early Christian hymn.
[4] Brunner, *The Mediator*, 562.   [5] Phil. ii. 9-11.
[6] *The Mediator*, 563.

significance. "Why seek ye the living among the dead?" [1] Why search for Christ in the wrong place? "Christian faith," writes Karl Barth, "is not to be understood as idealism that has succeeded in discovering light in darkness, life in death, the majesty of God in the lowliness of human existence and destiny. *Resurrexit* means—*Jesus* is conqueror. A Christian Easter sermon had best be silent over the longings and outpourings of human optimism. Christian faith is happy and confident because and in virtue of this fact, that Jesus Christ Himself acted, that is, *God* in Christ." [2] Therefore the all too familiar type of religious piety which admires and even worships Jesus as a great commanding figure of history, *primus inter pares,* which hails His influence and venerates His memory and lays wreaths of eloquent tribute on His tomb, is whole worlds away from the faith of the New Testament. And there is no true preaching of atonement until we can point men past the Cross and say: "He is not here. He is risen. Behold Him travelling in the greatness of His strength, mighty to save!"

IV

RIGHTEOUSNESS VINDICATED

If the first note in the apostolic preaching of the Resurrection was Christological, the second proclaimed *the vindication of righteousness.* For what the Resurrection meant to those men was this: "There

---

[1] Luke xxiv. 5. [2] *Credo,* 98.

is a power in action stronger than the whole hideous alliance of evil forces that crucified our Lord." They now saw that in the agelong terrible conflict of which history was the arena—that perpetual conflict between good and evil, light and darkness, God and the demons, which came to a head at the crucifixion— the last word lay with God. They knew now that they were facing a defeated enemy. The power which had taken Jesus out of the grave would yet remake the dark and ruined world, and smite dead hopes with sudden life. The Resurrection is not just a personal survival: it is a cosmic victory.

In T. S. Eliot's play *Murder in the Cathedral,* the priests bar the doors of the great Church of Canterbury against the would-be assassins. But Thomas the Archbishop, though knowing they have done it for his safety, will not permit it.

> Unbar the doors! throw open the doors!
> I will not have the house of prayer, the Church of Christ,
> The sanctuary, turned into a fortress . . .
> The Church shall be open, even to our enemies. Open
> the door!

And when they protest, thinking him reckless and mad and desperate, urging him—

> You would bar the door
> Against the lion, the leopard, the wolf or the boar,
> Why not more
> Against beasts with the souls of damned men, against
> men
> Who would damn themselves to beasts. My Lord! My
> Lord!

his answer rings out clear:

> We have fought the beast
> And have conquered . . .
> Now is the triumph of the Cross, now
> Open the door! I command it. OPEN THE DOOR!

This was the spirit of the apostles. God had fought the beast and conquered. Now was the triumph, and nothing could stand against it. The Son of God had been manifested to destroy the works of the devil, and this was the act which assured their ultimate destruction. However dark and menacing the forces ranged against the Gospel, the battle had been won. What had Christ's men to fear? Open the door—even to the enemy! For Satan as lightning had fallen from heaven.

To-day within the Christian ranks many are in danger of forgetting this.[1] Of course, it is not altogether surprising. The world has gone so mad and suicidal, perverting its glorious achievements of intellect and inventiveness with diabolical ingenuity to frightful ends, that men begin to ask "Are we heading back to the Dark Ages?" All very well to go to Church and sing—

> So be it, Lord! Thy throne shall never,
> Like earth's proud empires, pass away;
> Thy Kingdom stands and grows for ever,
> Till all Thy creatures own Thy sway— [2]

but do we believe it? Do we really mean it? What

---

[1] At this point, and on pages 125 and 129, I reproduce with certain changes a few passages from an article I contributed to *Man's Dilemma and God's Answer* (Student Christian Movement Press): I am indebted to the S.C.M. for permission to use these paragraphs here.

[2] John Ellerton.

about bacteriological warfare? What about the cleaving of the world into hostile camps? What about the misery of the millions of refugees? What about the perverting of the truth in those hatefully manipulated trials of Christian brothers of our own in Europe and the Far East? "Thy Kingdom stands and grows for ever"—does it? Or is that just the bankruptcy of intelligence, silly pretence, crazy rhetoric?

It comes strangely upon us to-day to reflect how easy our forbears found it to believe that history itself and man's progress in history could supply all the evidence necessary for the ultimate vindication of righteousness. There have been ages of which this mood was characteristic, times when the Christianization of the world seemed in sight; when, to quote Tennyson's dream, "mind and soul"—man's logic and his faith—were indeed "making one music"; [1] when progress marched with irresistible momentum. But we are learning now that thus to base the final victory of Christ simply upon the course of history is a precarious undertaking. For truth can be defeated in history, and the lights go out. As Professor K. S. Latourette has reminded us, "In the seventh and eighth centuries Islam tore away about half of what might be called 'Christendom,' and in that half were some of the oldest and strongest Churches." [2] Where to-day are the once great and illustrious Christian communities of Egypt and North Africa, where the seven Churches of Asia? In Europe and beyond there are lands virtually

[1] *In Memoriam.*
[2] *International Review of Missions*, Vol. XI. No. 158, p. 145

closed to the proclamation of the Gospel and the reaping of the missionary harvest, where the doors once stood wide open to the messengers of Christ.[1] The fact is that when Paul told the Galatians, "If righteousness come by the law, Christ need never have died," [2] he might also have added, "If the vindication of righteousness come by history, Christ need never have been resurrected." It took the Resurrection to give the proof that human history could never give. But that proof the Resurrection once for all proclaimed: so that now, in civilization's darkest hours, we still can say, "The darkness is not dark with Thee, but the night is clear as the day." [3]

I am not indeed suggesting that this is all that a Christian will have to say about the dreadful dilemma of social and international evil. I am not suggesting that he should be passively resigned, like the fool who murmurs idly: "God is on the throne—so everything is bound to come right at last." But I am assuredly suggesting that unless we can say this one thing first and foremost and all the time, there is nothing else worth saying. Unless we have seen God Himself going into action against the agelong mystery of evil, all our devices and debates are mere empty chatter.

But that we have seen. We have seen the eternal order suddenly breaking through; and in that flash across the midnight we have seen the divine invincible determination to bring forth righteousness to victory and make Christ Lord of all. "Thine is the

[1] Stephen Neill, *Christ, His Church and His World*, 114.
[2] Gal. ii. 21.
[3] Psalm cxxxix. 12.

Kingdom and the Power and the Glory." This is the secret of a brave heart in these faith-shattering days, and this we are commissioned to preach: "Remember Jesus Christ, risen from the dead!" [1]

V

GOD'S POWER FOR MAN'S WEAKNESS

There was a third note in the apostles' preaching of the Resurrection. They went to men enslaved by fierce pagan passions, defeated and battered and disillusioned, and they said, *You can share Christ's risen life!* "The God of peace, who brought again from the dead our Lord Jesus, that great Shepherd of the sheep, through the blood of the everlasting covenant, make you perfect in every good work to do His will, working in you that which is well-pleasing in His sight, through Jesus Christ." [2]

Thus to-day preaching the Resurrection means telling men that the identical divine energy which at the first took Christ out of the grave is available still —available not only at journey's end to save them in the hour of death, but available here and now to help them to live. As Paul wrote in glowing words to the Ephesians: the power of God in us "operates with the strength of the might which He exerted in raising Christ from the dead." [3]

This is the startling, magnificent truth we are commissioned to proclaim. It is an awful catastrophe for the Church when the proclamation of such

1 II. Tim. ii. 8.   2 Heb. xiii. 20, 21.   3 Eph. i. 19, 20.

a Gospel grows—God pity us—dull and listless and mechanical. That God, by the miraculous energy of grace, brought Christ through death and set Him on high is a victory to make the angels shout for joy. But that the same power which on that day shattered death is now given us for life—to vitalize the most depressed and disillusioned and defeated son of man into a resurrected personality and a conquering soul —this is a theme to wing our words and inspire our witness and thrill the whole Church with music.

This was the apostles' message. And lest any of their hearers should imagine they were being merely rhetorical and romantic, always these men of the New Testament went on to say—"We proclaim this for we have proved it! It has worked for us."

The truth of that claim is unmistakable. How was it that a little group of men in an upper room— ordinary, fallible, blundering men—became the nucleus of a movement that was to turn the world upside down? This was the Church's hidden secret. It was not that they were commanding personalities; most of them were not. It was not that they had official backing, impressive credentials, or illustrious patronage: of all that they had less than nothing. It was this—that the unearthly power which at the first had brought creation into being, which now at the last had inaugurated a new creation in the Resurrection of Christ, had laid hold upon them and refashioned their lives as with a second birth: "There is a new creation whenever a man comes to be in Christ." [1]

[1] II. Cor. v. 17.

Has this resurrection power, then, been with-drawn? Surely we are sent to proclaim that in Christ it is available still. And to the man who objects—"This power you talk of is not for me! I am not the stuff out of which God's Easter victories are made. Don't mock me with the mirage of Christlikeness. I know myself too well: my thwarting frailties are too baffling, the contradiction of my nature too in-exorable, the chains of defeat too firmly shackled on my soul"—the real New Testament answer is to say: "You surely do not imagine that the power which took Christ out of the grave is going to be baffled by you? That the God who did that colossal, pro-digious act of might is going to find your problem too hard for His resources? That He who on that great day broke the last darkness of the universe may have to confess Himself impotent on the scale of your life and say, 'I can achieve nothing here: this is too intractable for Me'? But that does not make sense," these men of the New Testament pro-test, "that doubt is utterly irrational! He who brought again from the dead the Lord Jesus, shall He not—to-day if you will ask Him—revive and quicken you?"

"Not for a moment," exclaims Karl Barth, "do we forget that our whole being and all our thoughts, words, and works are liable to utter damnation. But we ask: 'Who is He that shall condemn? It is Christ that died, yea rather, that is risen again.' It is because He is risen again . . . that we put that question so defiantly. With that question we are merely allowing God to be God!"[1]

[1] *Credo*, 103.

This, then, we are to preach. Christ is risen; and that man is more than conqueror who is risen with Him.

VI

THE UNSEEN COMPANIONSHIP

Still further, the apostolic preaching contained a mystical note, the message of *the unseen Companionship*. No serious exegete of the New Testament will dare to discount the frequent passages in which this finds expression. Are we to take the Pauline language of intimate personal communion with the risen Lord, and dismiss it as unrealistic and neurotic, the cliché of a religion whose emotionalism is stronger than its logic? Are we to exclude the evidence of all the men and women of nineteen centuries who have testified that in the fellowship of the living Christ they have found a force that transformed their lives? Not if we are honest with the facts.

Was it empty rhetoric when David Livingstone said it was not just himself who went tramping through darkest Africa: it was David Livingstone and Jesus Christ together? Was it fever or delirium when Samuel Rutherford wrote to a friend from prison: "Jesus Christ came into my cell last night, and every stone flashed like a ruby"? Was it credulity or distortion of fact that made a great scholar of this generation say, after visiting a friend in the Christian ministry who had worked himself almost to death in a Midland slum, that in that poor room

he encountered Christ: there was his friend living
in that hell, and there was Christ beside him?[1]

These things are fact. "If we have grown into
Him by a death like His," wrote Paul to the Romans
in a passage where his Christ-mysticism came to
fullest expression, "we shall grow into Him by a
resurrection like His."[2] This intimacy of communion with Christ, so central for Paul, is faith's
cardinal conviction in every age. I am not saying,
of course, that Christians must always have a vivid
feeling of "Someone there," or that the unseen
Presence was ever meant to be an uninterrupted,
immediate consciousness, a perpetual beatific vision.
But this I do know, and this I am sent to preach—
that Christ being alive, there is for everyone who
humbly seeks to do His will the opportunity of
direct communion with Christ Himself, and all the
marvellous reinforcement of personality which such
communion gives. And this also is in it when we
say, "Remember Jesus risen from the dead!"

VII

THE BIRTH OF THE CHURCH

From all this there emerges *the koinonia, the new
Israel of the Spirit, the Church.* This was the fifth note
in the apostolic proclamation. The Resurrection
Gospel could never lead to that religious individual-

---

[1] This encounter is described in a most moving passage of Canon
Raven's *A Wanderer's Way*, 83.
[2] Rom. vi. 5 (Moffatt).

ism which is the peculiar danger of the mystic way.
For those who had received into their hearts the
magnificent good news, those to whom union with
the risen Lord had become the very breath of life,
those who could say with Paul "Life means Christ
to me," [1] were now for ever bound indissolubly to
one another. There are contemporary theologies
which have failed to understand this sequence. They
maintain that the Christian community created its
message of a divine Redeemer. They take it as
axiomatic that the Church produced the faith by
which it was to live. Nothing could be more per-
verse. It was the Resurrection which, in the power
of the Spirit, called the community into being. It
was the wonderful good news that broke down, not
only the "wall of partition" between Jew and Gentile,
but every other barrier besides. It was the Easter
Gospel that fashioned the Church.

How could those upon whom the stupendous
revelation had dawned remain apart? They could
see its light in each other's eyes; they could read its
message in each other's lives. They were sharers in
the one incredible secret. Other men might inhabit
a nightmare-haunted, demon-ridden world: but
they knew the demons were defeated. Others
through fear of death might still be subject to
bondage: they had seen death lying dead. Belong-
ing now for ever to Christ, they belonged inevitably
to one another. Sharing in His life, they had dis-
covered the true *koinonia*. Fired with a consuming
passion to tell the good news everywhere, they were

[1] Phil. i. 21.

welded into one instrument in the hand of God. The
Easter event created the Body of Christ.

> Where He is in the heart,
> City of God! thou art.

I have indicated already [1] that the Resurrection of
Jesus in the New Testament corresponds to the day
of Creation in the Old. There God sent humanity
forth upon its long pilgrimage to the Incarnation;
here He makes a new humanity, and gives it a
mission that will never end till the Parousia. There
was the Logos, "first-born before every creature";
here is Jesus, "first-born from the dead," [2] the
Head of a great brotherhood which is the first-fruits
of a world redeemed. There the initial step on the
road to Israel, to the Remnant, to the Suffering
Servant, to a lonely Son of Man upon a Cross; here
in the Resurrection the first outward reach towards
the glorious company of the apostles, towards the
Israel after the Spirit, towards the Gentile mission,
towards the holy Catholic Church throughout all the
world. In every age, the man who has seen the
risen Christ is the man with a mission; his true
home is a missionary community; and God wills
that through him others may be drawn into the
fellowship. "That which we have seen and heard
declare we unto you, that ye also may have fellowship
with us: and truly our fellowship is with the Father,
and with His Son Jesus Christ." [3] From the Resurrection comes the Church, "fair as the moon, clear

---

[1] Page 106 above.   [2] Col. i. 15, 18.   [3] I. John i. 3.

as the sun, and terrible as an army with banners." [1]
From this great act of God she took her primal
being; and all the reviving well-springs of her
life are there.

VIII

Death, Where Is Thy Sting?

Now there is just one other thing. The final note
in the apostolic preaching of the Resurrection was
the defeat of death.

They knew, those people of the new covenant,
when death invaded their dearest and most precious
relationships, when this grim ruthless fact—man's
ultimate enemy, the mark of his fallen condition and
the wages of his sin—confronted them with its
merciless finality, they knew that death was no
longer the frightful contradiction of all human hope
which once it seemed to be. For their own eyes had
watched death's bondage being broken and the
darkness routed and the fall reversed. The sting of
death was sin, and the strength of sin was the law;
but now they knew that the sting was drawn, and
the strong tyrant reduced to impotence. No more
could sin threaten to sever the soul from God. No
longer could the law annihilate the sinner with condemnation and despair. They had seen One coming
back out of the shadows to tell them all was well.

> Death's flood hath lost its chill
> Since Jesus crossed the river. [2]

---

[1] Song of Solomon vi. 10.   [2] From " This joyful Eastertide."

What was there left to be afraid of? If at one point in history the tyrant's grip had been broken, then his reign was done. If One had shattered the myth of death's invincibility, there was victory for all. In Karl Heim's expressive figure: "Just as when a dyke in the Low Countries on the shores of the North Sea gives way, even if it is only one little section, we know that, although this is in itself an event of small importance, the consequences are incalculable: beyond the dyke is the tumultuous sea, which will burst through the opening—so Paul knew, when he had met the Risen One, that 'He is the first-born of them that slept'!" [1] What, then, had they to fear? "Behold," cried Stephen, when the stones began to fly, "I see the heavens opened, and the Son of Man standing on the right hand of God": [2] not seated now as in the vision of the Messianic psalm, but standing—as Chrysostom expressed it—"to reveal His succour to the martyr, even as of the Father it is said, Let God arise!" "This is my day of coronation," declared Perpetua, preparing to face in the Carthaginian arena the valley of the shadow of death. "This is the day which the Lord hath made," exclaimed James Guthrie the Covenanter, when the grey dawn of the day of execution came stealing into the condemned cell where he lay and wakened him from a peaceful sleep, "we will rejoice and be glad in it." This is what it means to "remember Jesus risen from the dead." This is the victory.

---

[1] *The Church of Christ and the Problems of the Day,* 157.
[2] Acts vii. 56.

Let us reflect that every time we stand up to preach to our congregation some are present who can never think of death save as a robber and an enemy, the despoiler of human hope and love; some to whom the march of the inexorable years and the pathos of mortality bring an inward deep resentment; some who have never been reconciled to life and providence since the day when death broke in and took their dearest. We can understand that mood. Nor let us forget those others who, whether stoically and philosophically or with bewilderment and deep disquiet, are facing a daily march which seems to them to lead nowhere in the end but to darkness and dissolution; those, too, perhaps whose spiritual discernment has perceived in man's physical mortality the token of the ruin introduced into the world through sin. This mood also we can understand. "Death," said Aristotle, "is a dreadful thing, for it is the end." We know how menacing that darkness can appear. Indeed, the New Testament takes death, not less, but far more seriously than Aristotle or any other philosopher who has grappled with the ultimate mystery. But we as preachers are to summon troubled hearts to listen—not to us, certainly not that—to God, speaking the word that can give beauty for ashes and make them serene in spirit about death and the hereafter: "Fear not! Lift up your hearts. Remember Jesus risen from the dead."

This, then, is our Resurrection *kerygma*, this supercharged, magnificent fact, "the glorious Gospel of the blessed God": and it is true. Whatever

CHAPTER FIVE

PROCLAIMING CHRIST

Not where the wheeling systems darken,
And our benumbed conceiving soars!—
The drift of pinions, would we hearken,
Beats at our own clay-shuttered doors.

Yea, in the night, my Soul, my daughter,
Cry,—clinging Heaven by the hems;
And lo, Christ walking on the water
Not of Gennesareth, but Thames!

FRANCIS THOMPSON, *In No Strange Land.*

THERE is one critical question which is perpetually haunting the minds of many who are seeking to serve Christ in His Church to-day. It is a question we often suppress, because it makes us uneasy; but it is too fundamental to be ignored. *If all the Bible says is true, why is our religion not accomplishing more?* Why is it not effecting a more radical transformation of the human scene? Why are our own lives not being delivered more thoroughly from compromise and defeat? Why is there not created a Church aflame with faith, free from the scandal of division, and inspired in all its members with a consuming passion to bear witness to Christ?

Here is this Book, packed full of the most glorious shining promises—promises which have been sealed by God's own hand and bear Christ's personal guarantee: "God is able to make all grace abound toward you"; [1] "the crooked shall be made straight, and the rough places plain: the mouth of the Lord

[1] II. Cor. ix. 8.

137

hath spoken it"; [1] "how much more shall your heavenly Father give the Holy Spirit to them that ask Him?" [2] "with God all things are possible." [3] Why is there such a difference between the promise and the actuality as we know it in our lives and see it in the Church and in the world around?

Here is the Gospel—the good news of a terrific force let loose in history for the redeeming of mankind. If that is there, why is mankind not redeemed? Why are we still struggling through the darkness of an age of blood and iron?

Here is the eternal love expressing itself in the immeasurable sacrifice of the Incarnation, in the vast compassion of Calvary and in the magnificent triumph of the Resurrection. Why is there not more to show for it in our own lives first of all and then in the world around? Why has this greatest drama ever enacted not had results, so far as we can see, anything like commensurate with the divine hope and dream behind it?

"Is this little," cries the Pope in Browning's poem, "all that was to be? Is the thing we see, salvation?" [4]

I

The Dilemma of Christendom

Now to-day there is no lack of voices claiming to diagnose this sickness of Christendom and to prescribe the remedy. Within the Church itself there

---

[1] Isaiah xl. 4, 5.   [2] Luke xi. 13.   [3] Mark x. 27.
[4] *The Ring and the Book*, X.

are many different notions of what we need most of all for the vitalizing of the faith.

Thus, for example, there are those who tell us confidently that our most urgent need is a restatement of the faith in intelligible terms, a rethinking of Christian doctrine and a clarifying of our dogmatic position.

Now admittedly there is room and scope for this. What God has done once for all requires to be re-explored by the best thought of every generation. And particularly, in this day of rival philosophies and formidable ideologies, it is essential that there should be a reasonable defence of the faith. It is a great thing to be able to show, as I believe we can, that intellectually as well as spiritually Christian doctrine hangs together and makes sense of the world; that, from the point of giving a rational account of the universe, there is more to be said for Christianity than for any of the alternatives.

I would indeed go so far as to suggest that in this matter it is high time we Christians stopped being diffident and apologetic and on the defensive, and carried the war into the opposing camp. The true strategy—when unbelief attacks our Christian faith and labels it credulity, the superstitious expedient of the unintelligent—is to draw attention to the towering, prodigious credulity of the critic himself. For, as that great champion of the faith, Robert Browning, pointed out long ago in *Bishop Blougram's Apology*, the intellectual difficulties in the way of consistent scepticism are ultimately more serious and insurmountable than those in the way of faith. "Just when we are safest," cries Browning, meaning just

when unbelief has successfully thrown off the last
clinging trammels of the spiritual interpretation of
life, and eliminated to its own satisfaction every trace
of a divine purpose for the universe, and secured its
position by a confident, impregnable dialectic—

> Just when we are safest, there's a sunset-touch,
> A fancy from a flower-bell, some one's death,
> A chorus-ending from Euripides,—
> And that's enough for fifty hopes and fears
> As old and new at once as Nature's self,
> To rap and knock and enter in our soul.

This clarifying of our dogmatic position, this pre-
sentation of the faith in intelligible terms, is an
important issue, and devoted toil and thought are
being given to it. Nevertheless, it is not the deepest
need. In fact there exists at the present time a real
danger of over-intellectualizing the faith—has one
not heard of a certain philosopher who was so busy
proving the existence of God that he forgot to say
his prayers?—a danger that the clamour of rival
schools of theology should drown the whisper of the
still small voice which is the living God. "Balaam,"
as Macneile Dixon reminds us, "though a man of
high intelligence, did not see the angel of the Lord,
but the ass saw him." [1] It is by no means an unknown
phenomenon—a theological intellectualism which
is spiritually sterile. There were Reformation theologians who, lacking Luther's saving experience of
personal encounter with God in Christ, narrowed
the horizons and rationalized into a Protestant
scholasticism the daring paradoxes of Luther's living

[1] *The Human Situation*, 390.

faith; and in every succeeding generation the danger has reappeared. But "the secret of the Lord is with them that fear Him." The child heart is still a better passport to the Kingdom of Heaven than religious and philosophical subtlety: and "dearer to God are the prayers of the poor."

Others have a different diagnosis. Our most urgent need, they declare, is not intellectual restatement; it is social emphasis. It is the recognition of the Gospel as social dynamite. It is the offer of religion as a lever for the regeneration of society and the refashioning of civilization.

This is a voice which we would do well to heed. If it was once a solitary voice crying in the wilderness —as for example in the days of the industrial revolution—it is this no longer. It is a great chorus now. Recent years have witnessed in all the Churches groups coming together to confer on the Christian answer to the challenge of Communism, and from such conferences two main results have steadily emerged. Two notes have been struck again and again. On the one hand, the Church has found itself confronted with the demand from its own people—"Give us doctrine! We must know where we stand. We must be really clear what we believe!" On the other hand, there has been the resolution—"We must integrate religion and life, and life means politics and economics and all the rest: we Christians must outlive and outlove the Communist in the realm of social passion."

Now all this is vitally important. No religion will ever represent the mind of Christ that does not throb

with social ardour and go crusading for a better
world. No faith deserves to bear the name of Jesus
which will not accept the risk, indeed the certainty,
of persecution in seeking to translate the doctrines of
the Fatherhood of God and the brotherhood of man
into the concrete vigorous action of a Christian
revolution, as it goes out to redeem the racially
disinherited and to establish the four freedoms
throughout the earth. The Bible itself is radically
outspoken about this. Bluntly it says, "Faith without works is dead." [1] Scathingly it cries, "You have
seen your brother, and have no love for him: what
love can you have for the God you have never seen?"[2]
"Inasmuch as ye did it not to one of the least of
these, ye did it not to Me." [3]

This goes very deep. "If a Church," declares
Brunner, "produces no living acts of charity for the
community as a whole, it is impossible to avoid sus-
pecting that she is sick unto death." [4] But I make
bold to say it does not yet go to the root of our
trouble. Indeed, here too there is a subtle danger—
the danger that we may come to value our holy faith
not for its own sake but as a means to an end, as a
contribution to some goal or consummation which is
regarded as more ultimate than itself. Thus Christ
as the absolute Truth is obscured. No longer do we
see overarching all secular history the judgment and
the mercy of the Lord. This is a matter touched
upon at an earlier stage in our argument,[5] and we
cannot pursue it further now. It will suffice to quote

---

[1] James ii. 26.   [2] I. John iv. 20.   [3] Matt. xxv. 45.
[4] *The Divine Imperative*, 558.   [5] See page 38 above.

these trenchant words of Bishop Lesslie Newbigin:
"There is a terrible danger that the Church should
become a large social service organisation with its
centre in a modern streamlined office rather than
God's family with its centre in 'the apostles' teaching,
and fellowship, the breaking of bread and the
prayers'."[1] Certainly a Church which yielded to this
temptation would be destroying not only its proper
witness but its potential impact on society as well.

II

THE DECISIVE RELATIONSHIP

What, then, is our basic need? If it is not a
reinterpretation of Christianity intellectually and
socially (though both of these, as we have seen, are
included), what is it? It is a rediscovery of Christianity as *a vital relationship to a living Christ.*

There is nothing so fundamental as this. The
longer one lives and the more deeply one ponders
the human dilemma, the clearer does this become.
I feel sure it needs to be said to-day quite unequivo-
cally that if, as Christians, we hope to grow in
grace and walk the way of faith and hope and love,
the prior condition is that our own life should be
interwined with the life of Jesus. Certainly apart from
this we shall never make the least impact on a secular
society nor arrest the drift to paganism, never even begin to save civilization and steady a staggering world.
The indispensable centre of Christianity is Christ;
and we ruin our religion if we centre it anywhere else.

[1] *A South India Diary,* 54.

I know, of course, that in a sense this is a truism. We have told men so often that "Christianity is Christ" that such words are now apt for many minds to have but little edge and bite. But the question remains—has it really been grasped that this is in fact what Christianity is, that (as Barth puts it) "Christianity does not exist for a moment or in any respect apart from Christ"? [1]

Many a time I have heard people discussing Christianity, or at least what they fancied was Christianity, criticizing, approving, patronizing it— apparently under the impression that Christianity is a compendium of ethical advice, an ideology, a philosophy of life, an amalgam of certain specialized virtues. It is true, of course, that if we Christians are to meet the challenge of the great formidable ideologies which to-day "bestride the narrow world like a Colossus," we must have a stronger, nobler ideology of our own. This is true. And we have it. But, if only we would realize it, we have something so much more than that, something which no other faith can claim: we have a living, eternally present Lord to set our hearts on fire, to love and to be loved by for ever. As Dr. John Mackay of Princeton has written: "A Christian filled with the Holy Ghost is the redemptive counterpart of the fanatical devotee of political religion. People consumed by the inner fire of the Spirit are the counterpart in human life of the smashed atom which releases cosmic force. It is not enough that I hear the Word of God and obey it. It is necessary that the Word

<hr>

[1] *Credo*, 159.

of God become incarnate in my flesh in a spiritual sense, that Christ be formed in me, revealed *in* me, and not simply *to* me. If there are theological dialecticians who declaim against piety and decry mysticism, so much the worse for them and their future leadership in Christian thought and life. What we need, in a word, within the Christian Church, if the Church is to match this hour, is Christians who are utterly Christian, in whom the full potentiality of spiritual life becomes manifest." [1] This is well and wisely stated. For the fact is that the burning focus of our faith is not the question, "What think ye of this or that or any other ideology?" but "What think ye of Christ?" [2] This is the centre.

And it really does need emphasizing to-day that what makes a man a Christian is not some vague pantheism or legalistic ethic or ecclesiastical affiliation, but the fact of his adhering to a living Person, Jesus.

III

CONVERGING LINES OF EVIDENCE

That this is indeed the indispensable centre and the beating heart of the faith can be shown from various lines of evidence.

Take, first, the evidence of Jesus' own repeated claims. There is nothing in the Gospels more significant than the way in which Jesus deliberately places Himself at the very centre of His message. He does not say with other teachers, "The truth is everything,

---

[1] *Theology To-day*, April 1946, p. 9. [2] Matt. xxii. 42.

I am nothing"; He declares "I am the truth." [1]
He does not claim, with the founders of certain
ethnic religions, to suggest answers to the world's
enigmas; He claims to *be* the answer—"Come unto
Me, and I will give you rest." [2] He does not offer
the guidance of a code or a philosophy to keep men
right through the uncertainties of an unknown
future; He says, "Lo, I am with you alway, even
unto the end of the world." [3] As Kierkegaard
expressed it: "All other religions are oblique; the
founder stands aside and introduces another speaker;
they themselves therefore come under 'religion'—
Christianity alone is direct speech." [4] There is no
question that if Christianity is to be true to the
intention of Jesus, it must be a relationship between
real persons. It is either this or nothing.

Take a second line of evidence. Call as witnesses
the men who were in it from the beginning. Take
the evidence of the apostles.

Suppose we interrogate Paul on this matter.
Intellectually, Paul was a giant. His synthesis of
Greek and Hebrew thought stands as one of the
most revolutionary achievements in the whole progress of human thinking. But the real secret of
Paul's terrific impact on history was not any such
original synthesis: it was the fact that here was a
man pervaded and possessed by Jesus. "To me,"
he cried, "to live is Christ!" [5] And again, "I live,
yet not I, Christ liveth in me." [6] That is Christianity:
a decisive relationship to a living Person.

---

[1] John xiv. 6.   [2] Matt. xi. 28.   [3] Matt. xxviii. 20.
[4] *Journals,* 52.   [5] Phil. i. 21.   [6] Gal. ii. 20.

Or suppose we interrogate a man of a very different type, Simon Peter. Peter was the stuff of which your flaming social idealist is made. Peter was a passionate reformer: the kind of man who is out to take the Kingdom of Heaven by storm, and to build a new earth in the shortest possible time. But trace that idealism, that passion, to its source and you come upon—what? Not upon some manifesto of the rights of man, not upon a summary of Christian social philosophy. You come upon this —"Lord, to whom shall we go? Thou hast the words of eternal life." [1] Or this—from Peter standing face to face with the representatives of political and ecclesiastical power—"There is none other name under heaven given among men whereby we must be saved." [2] Always that decisive relationship.

Consider a third line of evidence. Test this matter by the witness of the great hours of the story of the Church. You will find this extraordinarily significant fact, that the most shining pages in the long record of the Christian centuries have been those where men—perhaps after some period of utter deadness—have met Christ again travelling on some new Emmaus road, and have welcomed Him home and given Him their love.

There was, for example, the Church of the Catacombs. What was it that braced the heart and nerved the arm of that persecuted, martyred Church in the days of the fiery trial when all Hell seemed to have been let loose? The very walls of the Catacombs shout the answer: for there, inscribed and portrayed

[1] John vi. 68.   [2] Acts iv. 12.

all around, is one ever-recurring figure—Jesus the
Shepherd, Jesus the Fisherman, Jesus the Bridegroom, Jesus the Prophet, Priest, King.

Or take the Church of the Reformation. Where
did that great movement originate? Not, as is
sometimes stated, from a sudden upsurge of dialec-
tical controversy. Not from any outburst of partisan
emotion. It had its origin and authentic beginning
precisely where Martin Luther himself said that
every true Christian must begin. "Begin," he said,
"from the wounds of Christ."

Once again, we might cite the Church of the
Wesleyan revival. Methodism, we know, has always
had its characteristic organization, its social passion,
its high dogmatic theology: but you do not come
upon the real secret of Methodism—its glow, its
strength, its drive—until you have heard Charles
Wesley singing "Jesus, Lover of my soul! Thou, O
Christ, art all I want: more than all in Thee I find."
Always there is that decisive relationship to a Person,
always that passionate adherence.

"What the Church possesses," declares Dr. T. W.
Manson, "is not immunity from sin and error but the
abiding presence of Him who is the way, the truth,
and the life. She is promised not safety but victory."[1]

There was once a famous Church at Ephesus.
The New Testament has branded in a sentence the
tragedy of that Ephesian Church: "Thou hast left
thy first love."[2] But what has been the inmost
meaning and the glory of every great revival of
religion but this—that there the Church has returned

[1] *The Church's Ministry*, 75.   [2] Rev. ii. 4.

to her first love, and hailed the Bridegroom of her soul, and found "glad confident morning again"?

Take a fourth and final line of evidence. Take the record of the saints, the men and women of God in every age. You can go back across the centuries to men like Bernard of Clairvaux or Francis of Assisi; or you can come down to modern times, to men like Bishop Azariah of Dornakal, or Donald Fraser of Livingstonia; and you will find that, utterly different as such men have been in almost every other respect, always there has been one common centre of their life, one burning heart of their experience, a communion with—almost an absorption in—Jesus, a clinging to this living Person with every fibre of their being. He has been with them always, even unto the end of the world.

This applies, moreover, not only to such great distinguished heroes of the faith, but also to multitudes of ordinary people, men and women of holy and humble heart, known only to God. All the way, from the upper room in Jerusalem right down to the twentieth century and the ecumenical Church, there has been an unbroken line of men and women who have borne the identical witness.

> Ten thousand thousand are their tongues,
> But all their hearts are one.

Suppose for a moment (this, I am aware, is a wild flight of imagination, but it is worth essaying it) that Jesus Christ could be eliminated from the lives of these men and women; suppose you could send them away from Him to live in a world whose noise

and strife had never been hushed to hear the heavenly
music of the Advent angels, whose midnight had
never been pierced by the sudden splendour of the
Easter dawn; suppose they were left to fight their
battles beneath the banner of materialism, to live by
bread alone, and to walk their pilgrimage unaccom-
panied by the Friend of the Emmaus road—it would
be the most shattering of deprivations, far worse than
taking his freedom of speech from a Socrates, or the
sights and sounds of nature from a Joan of Arc.   It
would be like ordering them to breathe without air.
For Christ is the vital centre of their world.

> O Jesus, Light of all below,
>   Thou Fount of life and fire,
> Surpassing all the joys we know,
>   And all we can desire.[1]

There, then, is the evidence.   And with all that
testimony behind us, we must reaffirm that this is
the indispensable centre of the faith, this is what
Christianity fundamentally is: a decisive relationship to a living Person.

IV

A CHALLENGING CRITICISM AND THE ANSWER

But now I recognize that at this point there is one
challenging criticism which has to be met and
answered.   "Sheer emotionalism," it is said.   "All
this talk about a personal passion and communion—
it is just romantic untheological mysticism, muddle-
headed mawkish sentiment, with no relevance to the

[1] Bernard of Clairvaux.

dust and blood of life's arena, sure to collapse in times of strain and trouble. If religion is to make any impact on this atrociously needy world, it must divest itself of all that kind of thing and show itself realistic. No doubt such mystic flights are all very well for people who are made that way and happen to like that kind of thing—a legitimate if eccentric hobby; but they are certainly not for the plain man immersed in the practical business of life. A plague on your mysticism! Let us disentangle the faith from all these emotional embellishments, and concentrate on Christianity as a programme for the moral life."

It is a familiar criticism. But it can be answered.

I answer, first, that *history is against it*. It is not introverted emotionalism, this faith in Christ; for again and again it has held and gripped men in desperate times when hope was a dream, when the boast of progress was sounding brass and secular optimism a tinkling cymbal, and when venerated codes and standards and ideals have been crashing down in disillusionment. Now mere sentiment could never do that.

I answer, second, it is not sentimental, this faith —*for it means decision*. It means the courage of heroic choice. "You have not made much out of all these years," said one Devon man who had stayed ashore and grown sleek and prosperous and wealthy to another who had served in the fleet of Francis Drake. "No," said the other, "I've not made much. I've been cold, hungry, shipwrecked, desperately frightened often: but I've been with the greatest Captain who ever sailed the seas!" So here. Sometimes men have been torn to pieces by their Christ-devotion. For in religion there is an existential decision which can be the most costly thing in the world. Jacob wrestled with God's angel at Peniel, and became a prince—but he emerged from that conflict maimed and crippled. Paul met his destiny at Damascus, and it beggared and ruined his earthly prospects, led him to stoning, shipwreck, imprisonment, death: "I count all things but loss for the excellency of the knowledge of Christ Jesus my Lord."[1] "I have lost everything on this voyage: but I have been with the greatest Captain who ever sailed the seas!" Men do not face such things for a fiction.

I answer, third, it is not emotional indulgence, this faith of fellowship with Christ: for having Christ with you everywhere and at every moment—"I am with you alway, even unto the end of the world" —is *not the soothing comfortable experience which some imagine it to be.* It is unutterably heart-searching and disturbing. For it means that we are never alone. That Other is always present. He is present now. We are not discussing in these pages a third party who is somewhere else. He is here. He is always present. When we are inclined to relax discipline and take some line of least resistance— a kind of moral holiday—He is there then. When we have done things of which we should be terribly ashamed to think that they should ever come to His knowledge, He has been actually present and His pure eyes have seen it all. "For ever with the Lord" —a cheap emotional indulgence? On the contrary!

[1] Phil. iii. 8.

It is the most soul-searching experience in life: so that we have to cry, "Lord, have mercy! Christ, have mercy! Lamb of God, who takest away the sin of the world, have mercy on us all!"

I answer, finally, it is not emotion—for it is *a logical consequence of the Resurrection.* Look at this sequence—risen from the dead; therefore, alive for ever; therefore, our Contemporary; therefore, able to confront us face to face. This is not emotionalism: it is logic hard as nails. That is why the great Indian Bishop Azariah, when asked one day, "If you were in a village where they had never heard of Christ, what would you preach about?" answered without hesitation, "The Resurrection!" This is why surely the most explosive words that have ever shattered the cyclic rhythm of history have been these: "Now is Christ risen from the dead!" [1] This is why Wesley could sing—

> We have through fire and water gone,
>   But saw Thee on the floods appear,
> But felt Thee present in the flame,
> And shouted our Deliverer's name.

He is risen! He is not nineteen hundred years away. And when you say your prayers to-day, He is really there at your side.

V

WHEN THE CHURCH REDISCOVERS CHRIST

If we can recapture this faith, if we can find again this great encounter, think of what would be liable

[1] I. Cor. xv. 20.

to happen. Think of what would happen in the Church.

How vitalized the Church's worship, when she knows her Lord is in the midst! Think of the thrill of singing out with all the heart the great songs of the Christian ages, when it is Christ Himself to whom you are singing; the joy of celebrating the great festivals of the Christian Year; the expectant eagerness of coming up to the House of God quite certain that Jesus will be there, and Jesus you are going to meet! If this faith is lacking in the life of the Church, there is literally nothing that can make up for its absence. Venerable tradition, apostolic succession, the democratic voice of General Assemblies, efficiency of organization, crowded services, elaborate machinery—all are utterly vain, mere dry bones, apart from the Spirit of the risen Lord. It is this alone which makes any community of Christians a Church, and not just a benevolent institution or one more redundant society cumbering the ground. Who could fail to be moved to the depths by that word of Jesus: "Where two or three are gathered together in My name, there am I in the midst of them"? [1] If our earthbound hearts could be struck vividly awake to the significance of these words, how the lost sense of the wonder of worship would come stealing back upon us! How eagerly we should welcome every returning Lord's Day, like those excited folk in Galilee lining the roads where Jesus was expected to pass! With what heartfelt sincerity we should echo the psalmist's words, "Blessed are

[1] Matt. xviii. 20.

they that dwell in Thy house: they will be still prais-
ing Thee.   Blessed is the man in whose heart are the
highways to Zion!" [1]   How vitalized the Church's
worship, when Christ is in the midst!

Again, how reinforced her sense of mission!   In
every age it has been this decisive relationship to
a living Person that has begotten the real missionary assault upon the world.   See what it did for
Paul.   It drove him tirelessly across the earth.   The
great frowning mountain ranges of Asia were no
barrier to this man, for beyond them men were dying
without Christ.   Down to the shores of the Aegean
he came, and in the wind across the western sea
heard dimly and afar the cry of myriads without
hope and without God in the world.   Always as he
turned his gaze towards Corinth, Illyricum, Rome,
Spain, the Christ in this man's heart was yearning
with a great compassion over those sheep without a
shepherd.   Always there was that driving sense of
an unseen compulsion—"I must share this marvellous relationship!   Necessity is laid upon me:
woe is me if I preach not the gospel!" [2]   And to-day,
it is when the Church passes beyond debating about
Christ and really begins to see Christ, risen and alive,
Very God and Very Man, "Joy of loving hearts,
Fount of life and Light of men"—it is then that the
springs of evangelizing zeal and passion are gloriously
set free.   You do not then hear any longer that
carping, stupid, faithless question, "To what purpose is this waste?" [3]—but everywhere arises the
odour of the ointment from the broken alabaster

[1] Psalm lxxxiv. 4, 5.   [2] I. Cor. ix. 16.   [3] Mark xiv. 4.

box of an uncalculating devotion. How reinforced the Church's mission, when Christ is in her heart!

Once again, how clarified her unity! It is possible —this we all know from sad experience—for Christians to spend long hours discussing the things that separate them, in Church government and worship and doctrine, and not make much progress in spite of all the talk. If only we would spend a few hours occasionally warming our hearts at the fire of the things that unite us—the different branches of the Church telling each other the new discoveries they have been making of Jesus and His grace— how that broken framework of the *koinonia* would be welded together, one army of the living God at last, girded for the fight! "The fundamental anomaly," declared the late Archbishop William Temple, "is that any two disciples of our Lord should not be in communion with one another."[1] I am not saying that having Christ in the midst will level out our idiosyncrasies or stereotype our varying points of view; but it does make us see in our fellow-worshipper a brother for whom Christ died, and in Christians of a different denomination another regiment in the one great army; and there is no basis for unity comparable with that. "The multitude of them that believed," says the Book of Acts in a lovely phrase, "were of one heart and of one soul."[2] For back of all barriers and divisions there is a point at which Calvinist and Lutheran, Evangelical and Roman are basically one: "If any

[1] *The Church looks Forward,* 12.   [2] Acts iv. 32.

man be in Christ, he is a new creature." [1] "Who
shall separate us from the love of Christ?" [2] "Unto
Him that loveth us be glory and dominion for ever." [3]
How manifested the Church's unity, when Christ
is all in all!

VI

WHEN CHRIST ENCOUNTERS THE SOUL

These things would happen to the Church. But
think, finally, of the effect of this faith-union with
Christ on the experience of the individual. In particular, let the Christian preacher, the herald of the
good news of God, think of his own life being
interpenetrated with the very life of Jesus. Let him
think of the personal conviction out of which he is
to speak being suffused with that thrilling sense of
immediacy and intimacy and directness:

> No fable old, nor mythic lore,
>   Nor dream of bards and seers,
> No dead fact stranded on the shore
>   Of the oblivious years:
> But warm, sweet, tender, even yet
>   A present help is He. [4]

Let any Christian think of going out into the world
with the ultimate loneliness of his spirit for ever
vanquished because Christ is with him; of facing
life in the assurance that henceforth not for a
moment does he walk unaided and alone!

[1] II. Cor. v. 17.   [2] Rom. viii. 35.
[3] Rev. i. 5, 6.   [4] J. G. Whittier.

Think of the inner peace it would mean—its effect on frayed nerves and harassed brain and daunted spirit. We are apt in these days to be besieged by life's unbearable enigmas and battered by its frightening responsibilities. We feel like Peter when he climbed down out of the boat to go to Jesus, and found himself caught in the swirl of the angry waves. We tell ourselves it is absurd that we should even attempt to be Christ's witnesses in a world like this and with a nature like our own: for "who is sufficient for these things?" And then across our hectic fever falls the voice of calm: "Lo, I am with you alway, even unto the end"; and we know that, whatever happens, He is quite certain to be there. This is the way to peace, and to the consciousness of adequate resources. For it is no weak Christ with whom we have to do, but a Christ of power—stronger than the stress of life, stronger than the tyrant sins that seek to smash us, stronger in the end than death itself.

> These eyes, new faith receiving,
>   From Thee shall never move;
> For he who dies believing
>   Dies safely through Thy love.[1]

VII

Contemplation and Commitment

If we can rediscover such a faith! But can we? And how is it to be done? If the fact and the face

[1] Paul Gerhardt.

of Jesus have gradually faded from before our eyes, if the decisive personal relationship has been damaged by sin and carelessness and the march of inexorable years, how shall we recapture what has been lost? I close with two quite practical suggestions.

On the one hand, there is this. We must make a point of returning far oftener than we do to Bethlehem and Nazareth and the Cross and the empty tomb, pondering this Gospel in all its breadth and length and depth and height, its loveliness and majesty, its piercing pity and searching challenge. I know that the old-fashioned terms our fathers used —such as "meditation" and "contemplation"—are much disparaged in this hectic age; we are not ourselves shining examples of the immutable peace that is God's gift; but somehow we have to recapture the thing for which these words stood. The ministry itself is by no means immune from the fever and the fret of this restless hour; but in honour to our vows and our vocation we are bound to discipline ourselves to make time to company with Jesus in the Gospels, to stand with Peter at Capernaum listening to His voice, to kneel with Mary at His feet, to climb the green hill outside the city wall, to run with two breathless creatures to the empty tomb in the Easter dawn. This we must do, until wonder and devotion are reborn, and we can say—

> That one Face, far from vanish, rather grows,
> Or decomposes but to recompose,
> Become my universe that feels and knows.[1]

[1] Robert Browning, *Dramatis Personae: Epilogue.*

And the other thing is this. Let us open our lives to Him, by removing the barriers that habitually keep Him out. Let us turn ourselves over to Him, remembering that this is not the act of a day but the work of a lifetime. "The way of life," wrote that fine Christian philosopher A. E. Taylor, "does not merely begin as a *via crucis*, it remains as a *via crucis* all through."[1] And Brunner does well to remind us that "the fact that the *ecclesia* is called *militans* does not mean primarily that it must defend itself against the world around, but that every one of its members is permanently engaged in a struggle with himself."[2] For the giving of oneself to Christ is never finished, but always to be reaffirmed, with a new existential decision every morning and a fresh surrender every night, until one day death seals the offering and makes our commitment complete.

And if at this present time there is some new demand He is laying upon us, some sacrifice from which we shrink, some burnt-offering we are disinclined to make—shall we not remember the example, singled out by our Lord Himself as worthy of perpetual remembrance, of one who, possessing a lovely alabaster box of most precious ointment, did not hesitate when Jesus crossed her path to break it at His feet?

[1] *The Faith of a Moralist,* I. 224.   [2] *Man in Revolt,* 460.